The aims and purpose of this book by Bingo Aki

ABOUT THE AUTHOR

Bingo Aki is an artist. He was born in Hiroshima, Japan, in 1948. He graduated from Tokyo National University of Fine Arts and Music where he studied Japanese painting. After he graduated, Mr. Aki's works were displayed in solo exhibitions all over Japan. He also has a passion for picture books. He was awarded the Japan Picture Book Prize in 2009. Today, he partners with educational experts and creates all kinds of educational materials.

Creativity is the power to make something new. Our children can't be expected to develop a creative mind solely by attending school. Creativity is something that needs to be encouraged at home as well—and the earlier, the better.

Imagine academic ability is like a car. It will take children to places they need to go to in life. Creative ability, however, is like a jet airplane. Creativity will propel children into a whole different stratosphere. It will allow them to become as free as birds flying in the sky.

So, how do we develop creativity? And how does it combine with work? In my case, it's by simply doing and learning from my mistakes. I take action without waiting for inspiration. To begin, I prepare my pencil and paper and launch on a writing spree. I don't think; I just let my hands go. I work without resting. It seems that the brain spontaneously makes discoveries simply by thinking about a certain thing for a while. The brain seeks and ideas come. That is inspiration—the discovery of something new.

In order to develop creativity, concentration is just as important as inspiration. To use our earlier analogy, a jet airplane can zoom thousands of miles above the earth, but first it must gain enough speed to lift off from the runway.

One of the world's greatest inventors, Thomas Edison, said, "Genius is 1 percent inspiration and 99 percent perspiration." The same can be said for creativity.

I created these books to help children develop concentration skills and cognitive ability. All your child needs to take advantage of these books is a pencil. In doing these exercises, children will improve their concentration, and train their brains to seek and discover.

While using these books, children should try to improve their skills by decreasing the amount of time it takes to do the exercises. They will need to do the exercises over and over again, and strive to eliminate errors and mental blocks.

These books represent my inspiration and creativity. I believe that by using them, your child will likewise develop his or her own powers of concentration, cognitive ability, inspiration and, finally, creativity.

Records

To parents

• Time how long it takes for your child to finish each page and fill in your child's log below.

• Please compare your child's record at the beginning of the workbook to his or her time at the end. You might notice your child is becoming faster at finishing his or her work.

• When your child has finished each page, please offer lots of praise.

1 animals (matching 24)	**17** produce (matching 28)	**33** animals (matching 34)	**49** insects (matching 38)
2 animals (matching 24)	**18** flowers (matching 28)	**34** fish (matching 34)	**50** birds (matching 38)
3 animals (matching 24)	**19** insects (matching 28)	**35** produce (matching 34)	**51** animals (matching 40)
4 fish (matching 24)	**20** birds (matching 28)	**36** flowers (matching 34)	**52** fish (matching 40)
5 produce (matching 24)	**21** animals (matching 30)	**37** insects (matching 34)	**53** produce (matching 40)
6 flowers (matching 24)	**22** fish (matching 30)	**38** birds (matching 34)	**54** flowers (matching 40)
7 insects (matching 24)	**23** produce (matching 30)	**39** animals (matching 36)	**55** insects (matching 40)
8 birds (matching 24)	**24** flowers (matching 30)	**40** fish (matching 36)	**56** birds (matching 40)
9 animals (matching 26)	**25** insects (matching 30)	**41** produce (matching 36)	**57** objects (matching 40)
10 fish (matching 26)	**26** birds (matching 30)	**42** flowers (matching 36)	**58** objects (matching 40)
11 produce (matching 26)	**27** animals (matching 32)	**43** insects (matching 36)	**59** objects (matching 40)
12 flowers (matching 26)	**28** fish (matching 32)	**44** birds (matching 36)	**60** objects (matching 40)
13 insects (matching 26)	**29** produce (matching 32)	**45** animals (matching 38)	**61** objects (matching 40)
14 birds (matching 26)	**30** flowers (matching 32)	**46** fish (matching 38)	**62** objects (matching 40)
15 animals (matching 28)	**31** insects (matching 32)	**47** produce (matching 38)	
16 fish (matching 28)	**32** birds (matching 32)	**48** flowers (matching 38)	

 Great job! You completed the book!

1 Exploring the Zoo
(Matching 24)

	Perfect within 1 minute		Great within 4 minutes		Fair within 8 minutes
	Excellent within 2 minutes		Very good within 5 minutes		Satisfactory within 10 minutes
	Super within 3 minutes		Good within 6 minutes		Keep Trying more than 10 minutes

DATE   NAME   TIME

■ Circle the matching animals.

elephant tiger pig bear
squirrel lion gorilla cow
mouse leopard zebra
rhinoceros panda tortoise
rabbit
horse frog crocodile fox
mole
giraffe guinea pig wild boar hippopotamus

giraffe frog wild boar rhinoceros
crocodile tiger
squirrel horse panda rabbit
pig bear mole tortoise
mouse hippopotamus cow
lion fox zebra
elephant gorilla guinea pig leopard

Exploring the Zoo

(Matching 24)

Circle the matching animals.

DATE   NAME   TIME

pig horse crocodile giraffe tiger mole zebra mouse tortoise panda elephant gorilla frog cow guinea pig rhinoceros lion wild boar squirrel fox bear hippopotamus rabbit leopard

gorilla cow lion guinea pig bear pig leopard rhinoceros zebra squirrel hippopotamus fox crocodile wild boar tortoise mouse panda tiger rabbit mole giraffe horse frog elephant

3 Exploring the Zoo

(Matching 24)

■ Circle the matching animals.

	Perfect within 1 minute		Great within 4 minutes		Fair within 8 minutes
	Excellent within 2 minutes		Very good within 5 minutes		Satisfactory within 10 minutes
	Super within 3 minutes		Good within 6 minutes		Keep Trying more than 10 minutes

DATE   NAME   TIME

gorilla, lion, rhinoceros, squirrel, tortoise, horse, cow, tiger, pig, rabbit, frog, panda, zebra, leopard, mouse, bear, crocodile, wild boar, fox, guinea pig, mole, giraffe, elephant, hippopotamus

hippopotamus, horse, panda, squirrel, pig, lion, wild boar, leopard, mouse, zebra, giraffe, cow, bear, fox, tortoise, gorilla, crocodile, rabbit, frog, guinea pig, rhinoceros, mole, tiger, elephant

4 Dive into the Water

(Matching 24)

Circle the matching fish.

Perfect within 1 minute
Excellent within 2 minutes
Super within 3 minutes
Great within 4 minutes
Very good within 5 minutes
Good within 6 minutes
Fair within 8 minutes
Satisfactory within 10 minutes
Keep Trying more than 10 minutes

DATE   NAME   TIME

scorpion fish

catfish

salmon

sea horse

eel

swordfish

sea bream

tuna

angelfish

arowana

flatfish

ray

sunfish

shark

jack

bonito

carp

black bass

flying fish

loach

anglerfish

anchovy

goldfish

blowfish

anglerfish

eel

arowana

black bass

ray

jack

sunfish

tuna

loach

sea bream

anchovy

scorpion fish

catfish

flying fish

goldfish

bonito

salmon

blowfish

angelfish

flatfish

sea horse

carp

swordfish

shark

5 At the Farmer's Market (Matching 24)

Perfect within 1 minute	**Great** within 4 minutes	**Fair** within 8 minutes
Excellent within 2 minutes	**Very good** within 5 minutes	**Satisfactory** within 10 minutes
Super within 3 minutes	**Good** within 6 minutes	**Keep Trying** more than 10 minutes

Circle the matching produce.

DATE NAME TIME

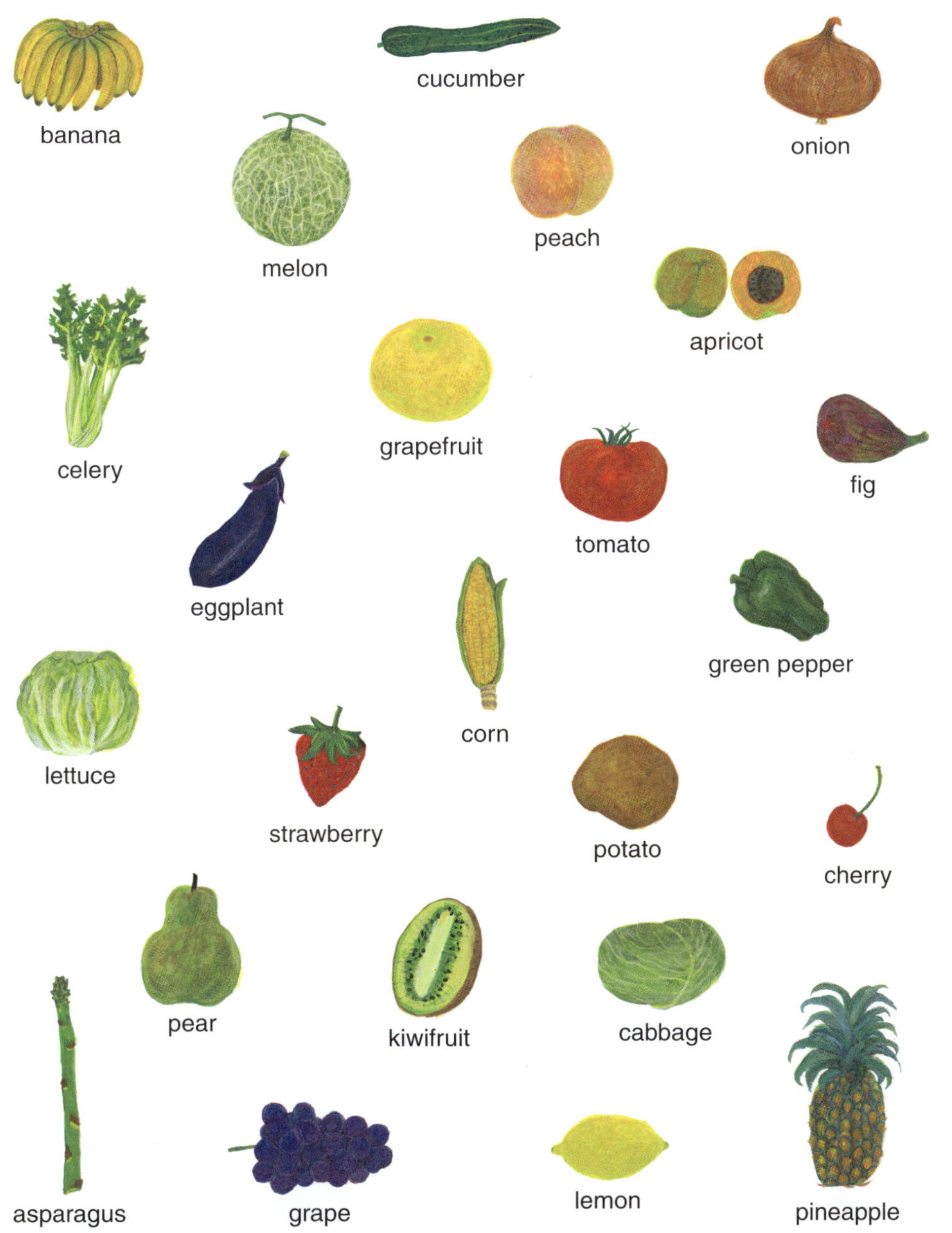

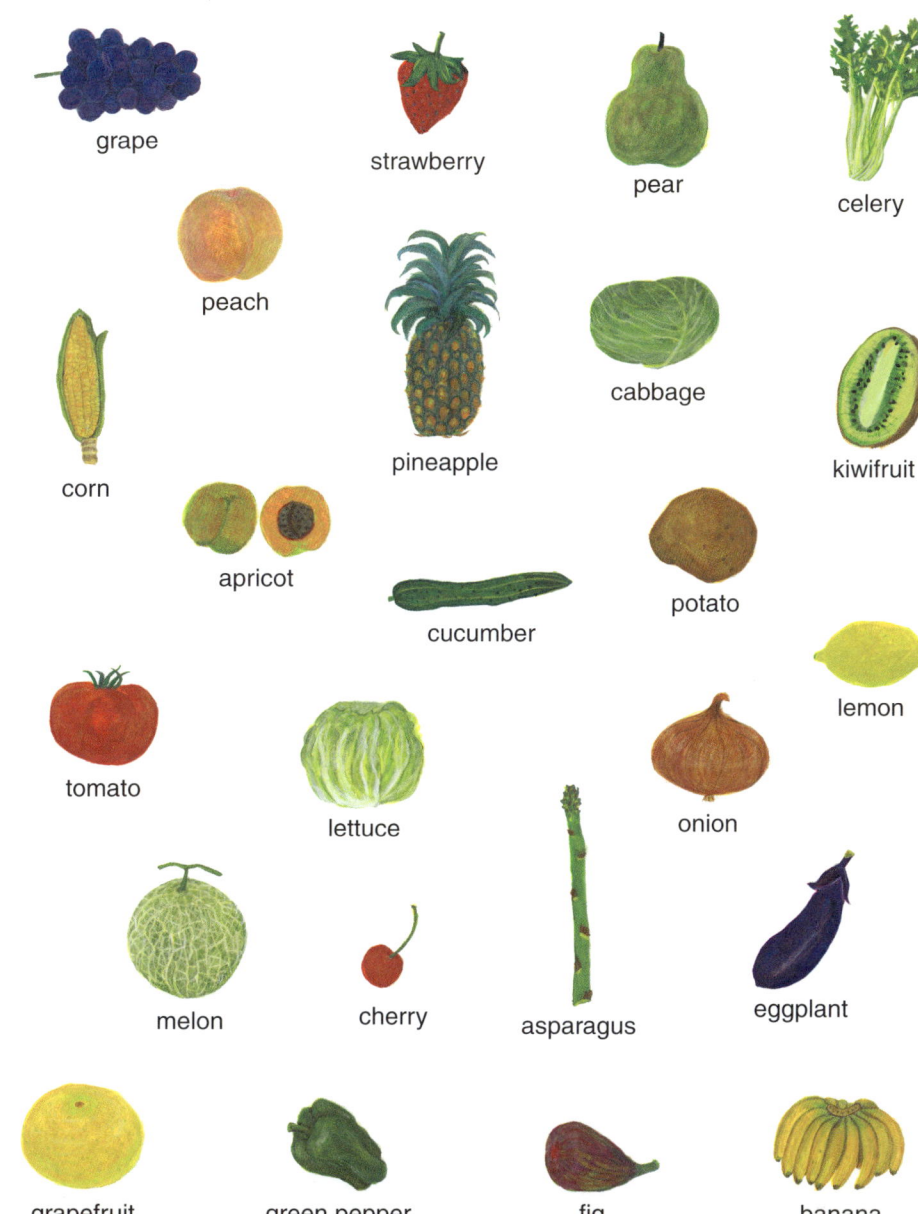

banana
cucumber
onion
melon
peach
apricot
celery
grapefruit
tomato
fig
eggplant
corn
green pepper
lettuce
strawberry
potato
cherry
pear
kiwifruit
cabbage
asparagus
grape
lemon
pineapple

grape
strawberry
pear
celery
peach
pineapple
cabbage
corn
kiwifruit
apricot
cucumber
potato
lemon
tomato
lettuce
onion
melon
cherry
asparagus
eggplant
grapefruit
green pepper
fig
banana

■ Circle the matching flowers.

DATE   NAME   TIME

gerbera, cactus, stock, poppy, anemone, sunflower, dahlia, rose, clover, violet, marguerite, lily, lily of valley, salvia, amaryllis, chrysanthemum, cherry blossoms, hyacinth, carnation, tulip, anthurium, dandelion, water lily, cosmos

clover, amaryllis, salvia, lily, chrysanthemum, hyacinth, dandelion, anthurium, cherry blossoms, poppy, dahlia, tulip, water lily, stock, sunflower, anemone, carnation, cactus, rose, gerbera, cosmos, violet, lily of valley, marguerite

🚀 **Perfect** within 1 minute	🚌 **Great** within 4 minutes	🚲 **Fair** within 8 minutes
✈ **Excellent** within 2 minutes	🚗 **Very good** within 5 minutes	🛴 **Satisfactory** within 10 minutes
🚁 **Super** within 3 minutes	🐎 **Good** within 6 minutes	🧗 **Keep Trying** more than 10 minutes

■ Circle the matching insects.

DATE   NAME   TIME

centipede

butterfly

locust

scorpion

long-horned beetle

stag beetle

ladybug

cricket

cicada

dragonfly

cockroach

water strider

mole cricket

katydid

fly

cricket

rhinoceros beetle

carabid beetle

firefly

bee

spider

grasshopper

jewel beetle

ant

spider

stag beetle

mole cricket

fly

ladybug

dragonfly

bee

centipede

rhinoceros beetle

cricket

cockroach

locust

cricket

jewel beetle

katydid

cicada

scorpion

grasshopper

ant

long-horned beetle

water strider

firefly

carabid beetle

butterfly

Birds of a Feather Stay Together (Matching 24)

■ Circle the matching birds.

DATE   NAME   TIME

penguin · crow · wild duck · pigeon · eagle · canary · magpie · pelican · goose · hawk · sea gull · turkey · ostrich · sparrow · swallow · swan · kingfisher · chicken · woodpecker · parrot · owl · flamingo · peacock · duck

owl · canary · turkey · crow · ostrich · magpie · pigeon · wild duck · swallow · eagle · chicken · flamingo · pelican · parrot · sparrow · peacock · woodpecker · kingfisher · goose · duck · penguin · swan · sea gull · hawk

Exploring the Zoo

(Matching 26)

■ Circle the matching animals.

🚀 **Perfect** within 1 minute	🚌 **Great** within 4 minutes	🚲 **Fair** within 8 minutes
✈ **Excellent** within 2 minutes	🚗 **Very good** within 5 minutes	🛹 **Satisfactory** within 10 minutes
🚁 **Super** within 3 minutes	🏇 **Good** within 6 minutes	🏃 **Keep Trying** more than 10 minutes

DATE   NAME   TIME

elephant zebra tiger giraffe
cow tortoise mouse
squirrel panda frog leopard
lion wild boar mole rabbit
  crocodile horse
gorilla cheetah pig
kangaroo rhinoceros guinea pig hippopotamus fox bear

gorilla kangaroo hippopotamus rhinoceros
squirrel cheetah rabbit zebra
tiger horse wild boar tortoise
mouse fox
elephant frog mole
  pig lion
cow crocodile
leopard panda guinea pig bear giraffe

■ Circle the matching fish.

	Perfect within 1 minute		Great within 4 minutes		Fair within 8 minutes
	Excellent within 2 minutes		Very good within 5 minutes		Satisfactory within 10 minutes
	Super within 3 minutes		Good within 6 minutes		Keep Trying more than 10 minutes

DATE　　　　NAME　　　　TIME

hammerhead shark　flatfish　swordfish

salmon　sea horse　sole

sunfish　sea bream　eel　shark

carp　angelfish　bonito　loach

scorpion fish　flying fish　anglerfish　tuna　jack

black bass　goldfish　catfish

ray　blowfish　anchovy　arowana

sole　goldfish　angelfish　sea horse

swordfish　eel　flying fish

carp　loach　tuna　jack

shark　sea bream　salmon

sunfish　scorpion fish　catfish　bonito

ray　anchovy　blowfish　arowana

hammerhead shark　flatfish　black bass　anglerfish

DATE   NAME   TIME

■ Circle the matching produce.

carrot

pineapple

grape

eggplant

broccoli

green pepper

grapefruit

celery

corn

banana

potato

apricot

cherry

asparagus

lettuce

fig

peach

cabbage

melon

cucumber

kiwifruit

tomato

onion

lemon

pear

strawberry

onion

cucumber

green pepper

broccoli

pear

carrot

grape

potato

banana

eggplant

apricot

corn

celery

melon

cabbage

peach

cherry

strawberry

tomato

lettuce

pineapple

kiwifruit

fig

asparagus

lemon

grapefruit

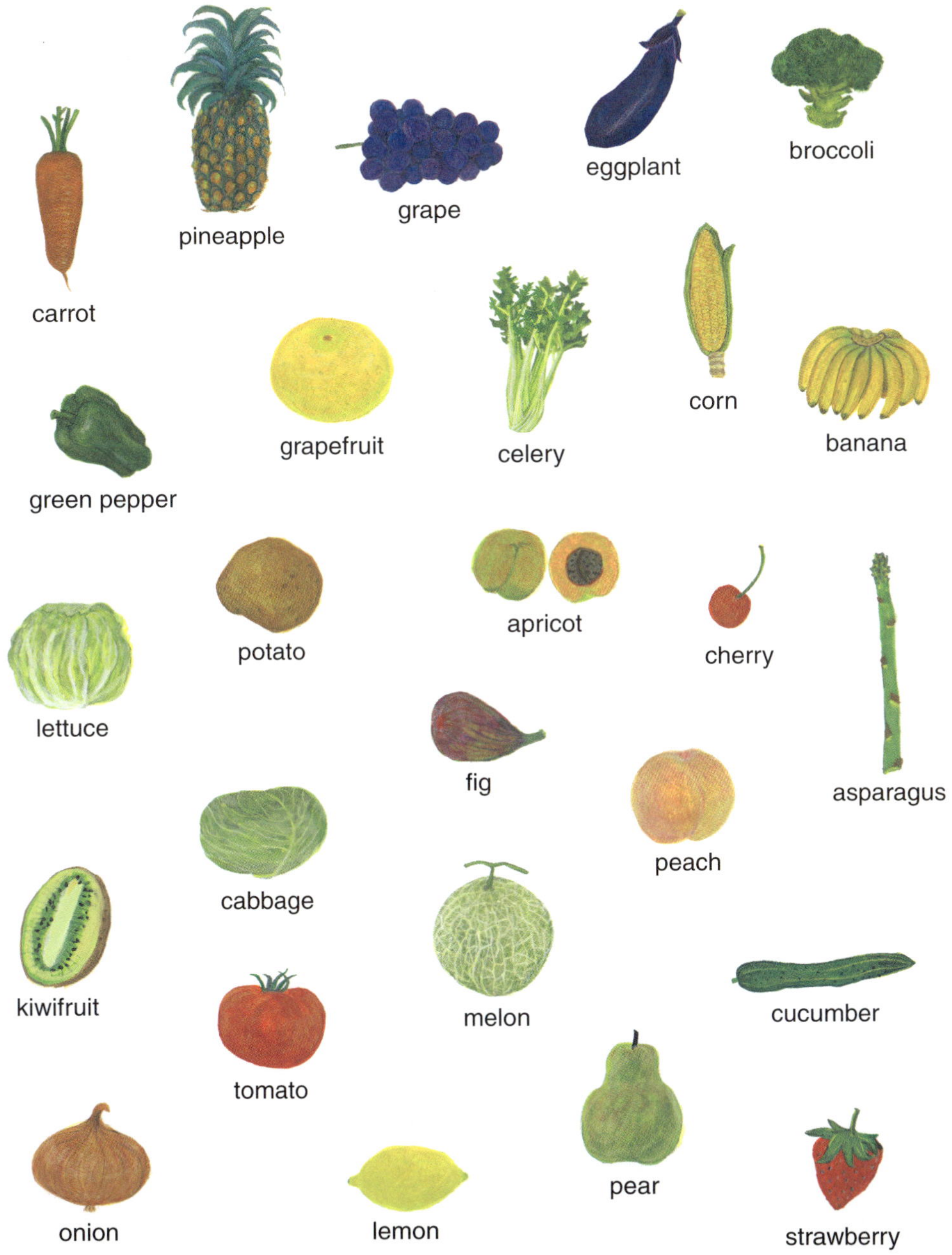

■ Circle the matching flowers.

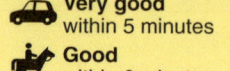

Perfect within 1 minute	**Great** within 4 minutes	**Fair** within 8 minutes
Excellent within 2 minutes	**Very good** within 5 minutes	**Satisfactory** within 10 minutes
Super within 3 minutes	**Good** within 6 minutes	**Keep Trying** more than 10 minutes

DATE   NAME   TIME

salvia, carnation, marguerite, hyacinth, violet, dandelion, poppy, gladiolus, sunflower, anemone, stock, rose, gerbera, rose, water lily, cactus, lily of valley, cosmos, clover, amaryllis, pansy, lily, chrysanthemum, dahlia, tulip, cherry blossoms, anthurium

cosmos, gladiolus, water lily, anthurium, pansy, cherry blossoms, lily, tulip, chrysanthemum, clover, violet, poppy, salvia, gerbera, stock, dahlia, rose, anemone, amaryllis, marguerite, lily of valley, sunflower, cactus, hyacinth, carnation, dandelion

Circle the matching insects.

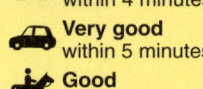

Perfect within 1 minute	**Great** within 4 minutes	**Fair** within 8 minutes
Excellent within 2 minutes	**Very good** within 5 minutes	**Satisfactory** within 10 minutes
Super within 3 minutes	**Good** within 6 minutes	**Keep Trying** more than 10 minutes

DATE   NAME   TIME

long-horned beetle

fly

dragonfly

grasshopper

butterfly

bee

moth

carabid beetle

mole cricket

ant lion

firefly

scorpion

spider

rhinoceros beetle

locust

cicada

jewel beetle

ant

cockroach

ladybug

cricket

centipede

water strider

katydid

cricket

stag beetle

rhinoceros beetle

spider

cricket

cicada

ant lion

stag beetle

locust

fly

jewel beetle

centipede

bee

cockroach

scorpion

ladybug

firefly

grasshopper

ant

carabid beetle

mole cricket

water strider

dragonfly

cricket

moth

butterfly

katydid

long-horned beetle

■ Circle the matching birds.

	Perfect within 1 minute		Great within 4 minutes		Fair within 8 minutes
	Excellent within 2 minutes		Very good within 5 minutes		Satisfactory within 10 minutes
	Super within 3 minutes		Good within 6 minutes		Keep Trying more than 10 minutes

DATE   NAME   TIME

flamingo
hawk
goose
peacock

swan
sea gull
magpie
sparrow

parrot
mandarin duck
duck
penguin
toucan

owl
canary
woodpecker
wild duck
chicken

kingfisher
swallow
pigeon
crow

ostrich
turkey
pelican
eagle

owl
toucan
turkey
crow
ostrich

wild duck
canary
magpie
pigeon

swallow
eagle
chicken
flamingo

pelican
sparrow
peacock

woodpecker
parrot
kingfisher
goose
mandarin duck

penguin
swan
sea gull
hawk
duck

15 Exploring the Zoo
(Matching 28)

■ Circle the matching animals.

	Perfect within 1 minute		Great within 4 minutes		Fair within 8 minutes
Excellent within 2 minutes		Very good within 5 minutes		Satisfactory within 10 minutes
Super within 3 minutes		Good within 6 minutes		Keep Trying more than 10 minutes

DATE　　　NAME　　　TIME

chimpanzee　elephant　horse　wild boar　panda　squirrel　pig　rhinoceros

lion

frog　leopard　tiger　fox　cow　bear　frog　cheetah

cheetah　hippopotamus　koala　mole　crocodile　giraffe　chimpanzee

kangaroo　tortoise　squirrel　zebra　lion　gorilla

mouse

zebra　gorilla　panda　guinea pig　horse　wild boar　crocodile　mouse　koala

pig　cow　tortoise　rabbit　tiger　mole　kangaroo　rabbit

giraffe　rhinoceros　elephant　leopard　guinea pig　fox　bear　hippopotamus

Circle the matching fish.

	Perfect within 1 minute		Great within 4 minutes		Fair within 8 minutes
	Excellent within 2 minutes		Very good within 5 minutes		Satisfactory within 10 minutes
	Super within 3 minutes		Good within 6 minutes		Keep Trying more than 10 minutes

DATE　　　　　NAME　　　　　TIME

flatfish

sole

ray

shark

sea horse

hammerhead shark

angelfish

carp

sunfish

sea bream

arowana

flying fish

goldfish

ray

salmon

catfish

sea horse

anglerfish

tuna

eel

bonito

sea bream

arowana

carp

bonito

anchovy

black bass

shark

loach

blowfish

scorpion fish

angelfish

cod fish

salmon

catfish

anchovy

flatfish

cod fish

coelacanth

black bass

blowfish

scorpion fish

jack

swordfish

swordfish

loach

sole

tuna

eel

hammerhead shark

jack

sunfish

anglerfish

flying fish

goldfish

coelacanth

 **Perfect** within 1 minute	 **Great** within 4 minutes	 **Fair** within 8 minutes
Excellent within 2 minutes	**Very good** within 5 minutes	**Satisfactory** within 10 minutes
Super within 3 minutes	**Good** within 6 minutes	**Keep Trying** more than 10 minutes

DATE   NAME   TIME

pear   tomato   green pepper   carrot   broccoli   lettuce   apricot   peach   grapefruit

cherry   lemon   banana   potato   onion   kiwifruit   tomato   pear   cucumber

asparagus   cucumber   fig   eggplant   corn   celery   green pepper   pineapple   grape   celery   strawberry   lemon

melon   grapefruit   walnut   apricot   apple   potato   melon   walnut   asparagus

melon   kiwifruit   strawberry   peach   grape   carrot   eggplant   cabbage   cherry

pineapple   lettuce   onion   cabbage   apple   fig   broccoli   corn   banana

■ Circle the matching flowers.

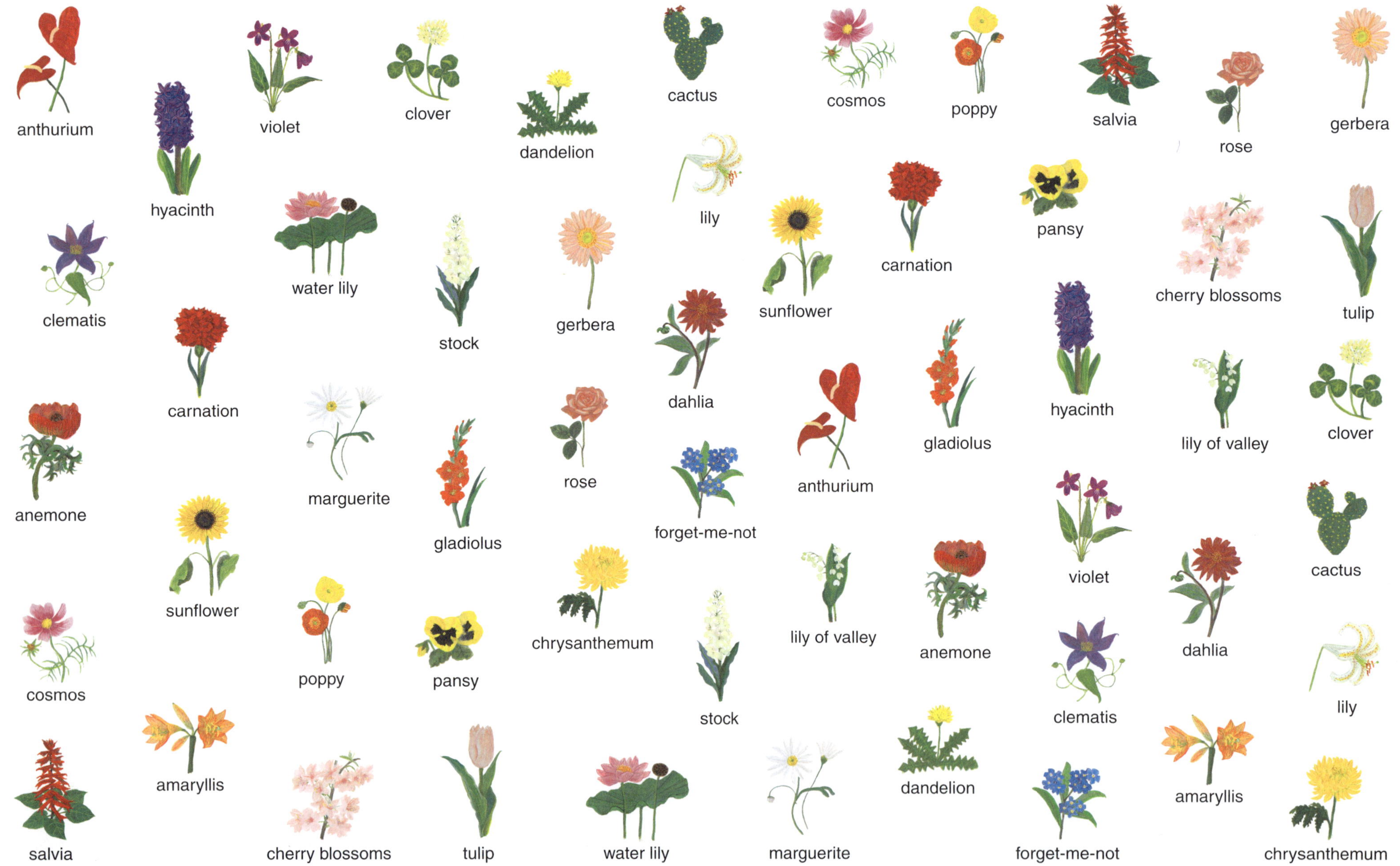

DATE   NAME   TIME

anthurium

hyacinth

violet

clover

dandelion

cactus

cosmos

poppy

salvia

rose

gerbera

clematis

water lily

stock

gerbera

lily

sunflower

carnation

pansy

cherry blossoms

tulip

carnation

marguerite

gladiolus

rose

dahlia

anthurium

gladiolus

hyacinth

lily of valley

clover

anemone

sunflower

poppy

pansy

chrysanthemum

forget-me-not

lily of valley

violet

anemone

dahlia

cactus

clematis

cosmos

stock

lily

 salvia

 amaryllis

 cherry blossoms

 tulip

 water lily

   marguerite

 dandelion

 forget-me-not

 amaryllis

chrysanthemum

19 Catch the Bug

(Matching 28)

Circle the matching insects.

Perfect within 1 minute	**Great** within 4 minutes	**Fair** within 8 minutes
Excellent within 2 minutes	**Very good** within 5 minutes	**Satisfactory** within 10 minutes
Super within 3 minutes	**Good** within 6 minutes	**Keep Trying** more than 10 minutes

DATE NAME TIME

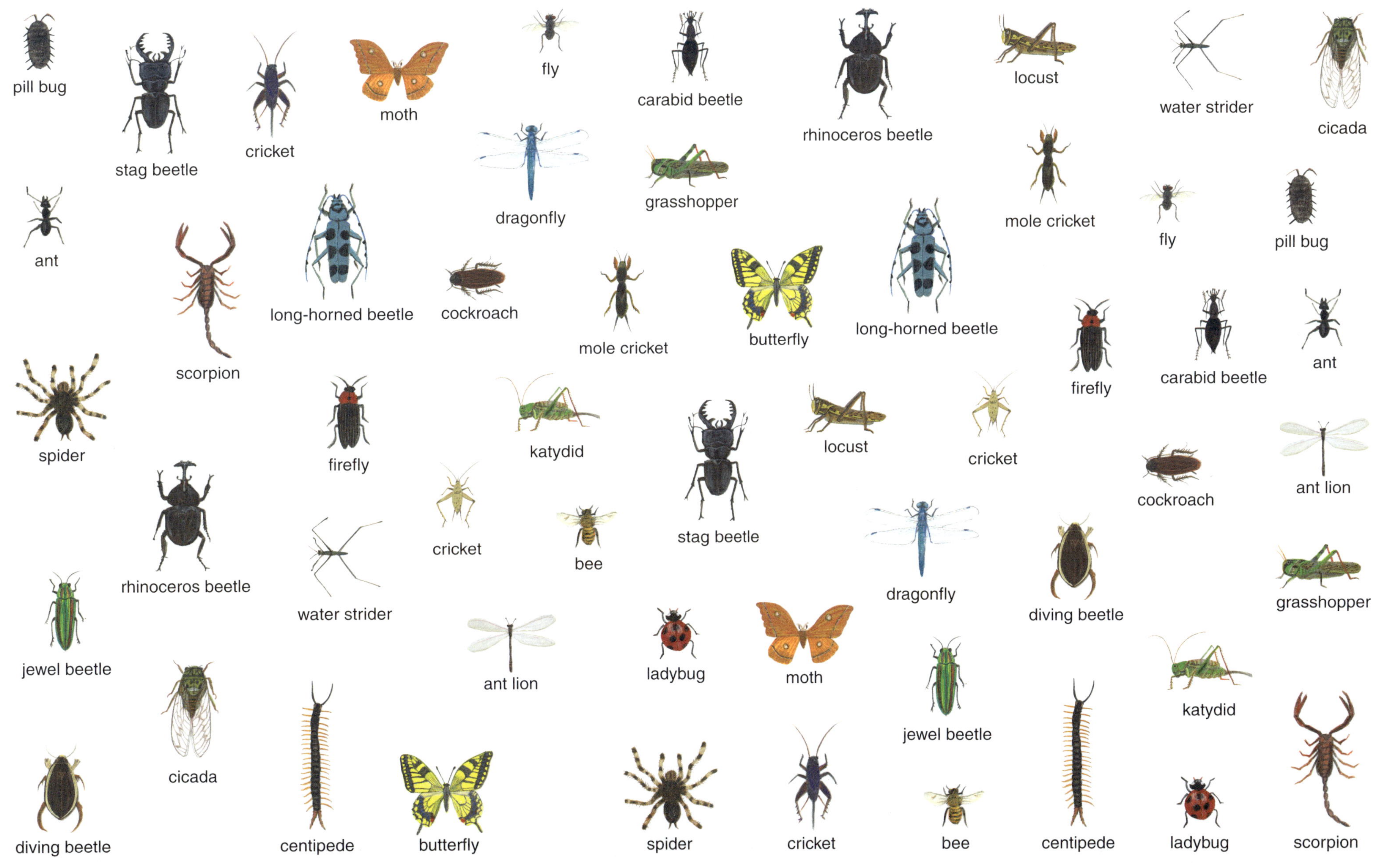

pill bug
stag beetle
cricket
moth
fly
carabid beetle
rhinoceros beetle
locust
water strider
cicada
dragonfly
grasshopper
mole cricket
ant
fly
pill bug
scorpion
long-horned beetle
cockroach
mole cricket
butterfly
long-horned beetle
firefly
carabid beetle
ant
spider
firefly
katydid
locust
cricket
cockroach
ant lion
rhinoceros beetle
cricket
bee
stag beetle
water strider
dragonfly
diving beetle
grasshopper
jewel beetle
ant lion
ladybug
moth
jewel beetle
katydid
cicada
diving beetle
centipede
butterfly
spider
cricket
bee
centipede
ladybug
scorpion

20 Birds of a Feather Stay Together (Matching 28)

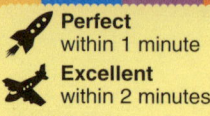

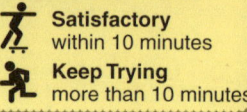

Perfect within 1 minute	**Great** within 4 minutes	**Fair** within 8 minutes
Excellent within 2 minutes	**Very good** within 5 minutes	**Satisfactory** within 10 minutes
Super within 3 minutes	**Good** within 6 minutes	**Keep Trying** more than 10 minutes

DATE NAME TIME

Circle the matching birds.

wild goose
scops owl
eagle
pigeon
swan
ostrich
toucan
woodpecker
pigeon
peacock
parrot
goose
toucan
penguin
magpie
chicken
crow
scops owl
pelican
magpie
canary
crow
sea gull
sparrow
turkey
wild duck
swan
owl
mandarin duck
kingfisher
swallow
duck
owl
sea gull
turkey
kingfisher
goose
wild duck
chicken
hawk
canary
parrot
swallow
mandarin duck
flamingo
duck
ostrich
peacock
flamingo
woodpecker
wild goose
sparrow
eagle
hawk
pelican
penguin

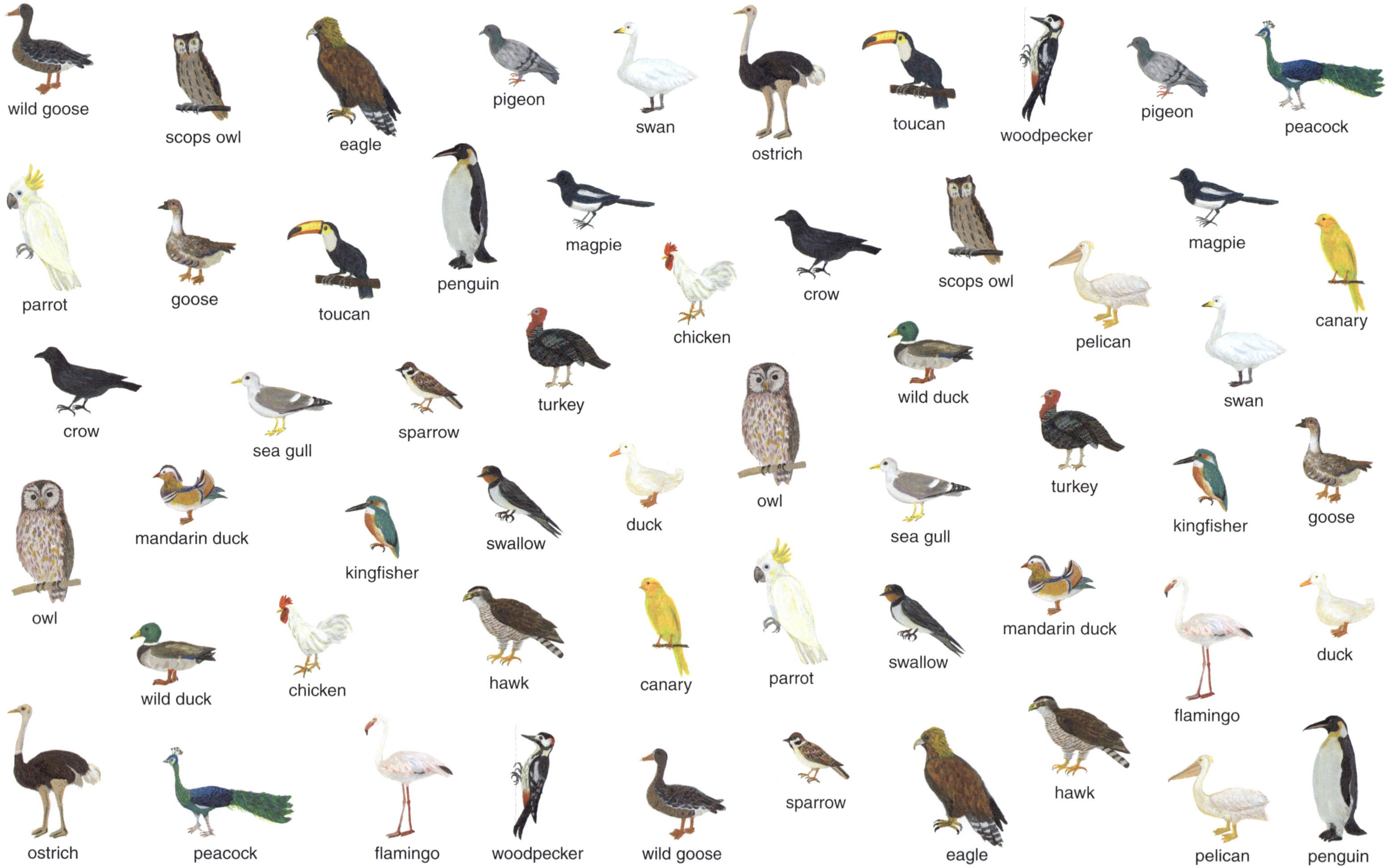

■ Circle the matching animals.

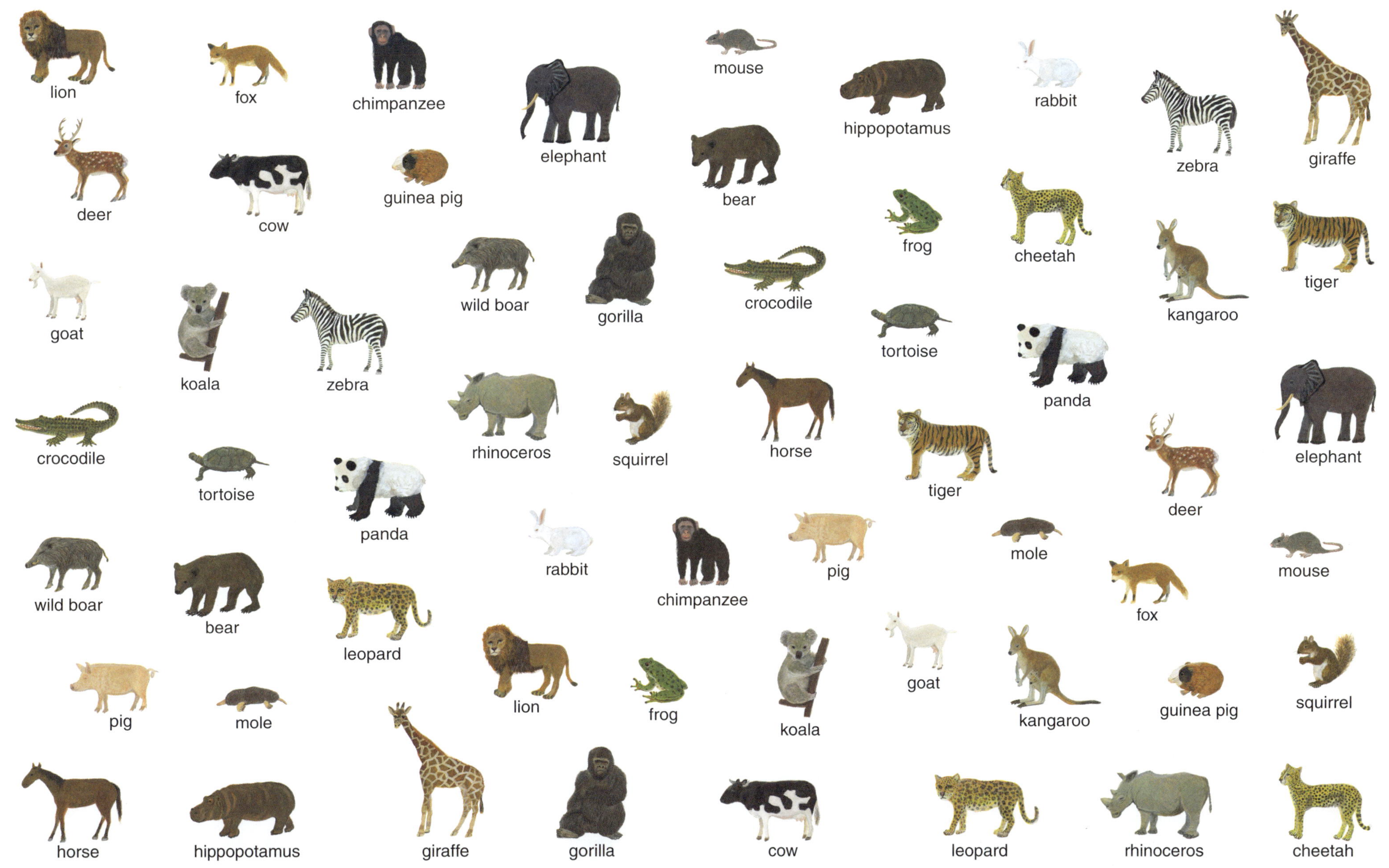

🚀 **Perfect** within 1 minute, 30 seconds	🚌 **Great** within 4 minutes, 30 seconds	🚲 **Fair** within 9 minutes
✈ **Excellent** within 2 minutes, 30 seconds	🚗 **Very good** within 5 minutes, 30 seconds	⛸ **Satisfactory** within 11 minutes
🚁 **Super** within 3 minutes, 30 seconds	🏇 **Good** within 7 minutes	🏃 **Keep Trying** more than 11 minutes

DATE   NAME   TIME

lion

fox

chimpanzee

mouse

elephant

hippopotamus

rabbit

zebra

giraffe

deer

cow

guinea pig

bear

frog

cheetah

goat

koala

zebra

wild boar

gorilla

crocodile

tortoise

kangaroo

tiger

crocodile

tortoise

panda

rhinoceros

squirrel

horse

tiger

panda

deer

elephant

wild boar

bear

leopard

rabbit

chimpanzee

pig

mole

fox

mouse

pig

mole

lion

frog

koala

goat

kangaroo

guinea pig

squirrel

horse

hippopotamus

giraffe

gorilla

cow

leopard

rhinoceros

cheetah

(Matching 30)

DATE   NAME   TIME

■ Circle the matching fish.

arowana

shark

scorpion fish

sunfish

sea bream

angelfish

sea horse

coelacanth

sole

swordfish

flying fish

porcupine fish

sea horse

flatfish

goldfish

anglerfish

cod fish

carp

hammerhead shark

cutlassfish

carp

coelacanth

ray

bonito

arowana

loach

salmon

bonito

angelfish

blowfish

sea bream

catfish

goldfish

shark

jack

anglerfish

sunfish

black bass

jack

eel

tuna

sole

black bass

flying fish

anchovy

swordfish

porcupine fish

catfish

salmon

scorpion fish

eel

cod fish

cutlassfish

hammerhead shark

anchovy

loach

ray

blowfish

tuna

flatfish

At the Farmer's Market (Matching 30)

🚀 **Perfect** within 1 minute, 30 seconds
✈️ **Excellent** within 2 minutes, 30 seconds
🚁 **Super** within 3 minutes, 30 seconds
🚌 **Great** within 4 minutes, 30 seconds
🚗 **Very good** within 5 minutes, 30 seconds
🐴 **Good** within 7 minutes
🚲 **Fair** within 9 minutes
🛹 **Satisfactory** within 11 minutes
🏃 **Keep Trying** more than 11 minutes

DATE NAME TIME

■ Circle the matching produce.

24 Picking Flowers

(Matching 30)

■ Circle the matching flowers.

	Perfect within 1 minute, 30 seconds		Great within 4 minutes, 30 seconds		Fair within 9 minutes
	Excellent within 2 minutes, 30 seconds		Very good within 5 minutes, 30 seconds		Satisfactory within 11 minutes
	Super within 3 minutes, 30 seconds		Good within 7 minutes		Keep Trying more than 11 minutes

DATE   NAME   TIME

rose, sunflower, amaryllis, clematis, marguerite, pansy, lily, anemone, poppy, sweet pea, clover

hyacinth, tulip, gladiolus, cosmos, cactus, salvia, lily of valley, stock, forget-me-not, dahlia, dandelion, cherry blossoms, gerbera, chrysanthemum, anthurium, rose, water lily, carnation, lily of valley

dahlia, cherry blossoms, violet, cosmos, lily, amaryllis, violet, persian buttercup

forget-me-not, carnation, stock, gerbera, clover, poppy, cactus, tulip, sunflower, hyacinth, gladiolus, anemone

persian buttercup, water lily, sweet pea, dandelion, pansy, marguerite, anthurium, chrysanthemum, clematis, salvia

25 Catch the Bug
(Matching 30)

Circle the matching insects.

	Perfect within 1 minute, 30 seconds	Great within 4 minutes, 30 seconds	Fair within 9 minutes
	Excellent within 2 minutes, 30 seconds	Very good within 5 minutes, 30 seconds	Satisfactory within 11 minutes
	Super within 3 minutes, 30 seconds	Good within 7 minutes	Keep Trying more than 11 minutes

DATE   NAME   TIME

scorpion

stag beetle

dragonfly

ladybug

ant

carabid beetle

moth

stag beetle

long-horned beetle

centipede

stick insect

diving beetle

ant lion

spider

rhinoceros beetle

grasshopper

ant lion

water strider

ant

butterfly

katydid

grasshopper

bee

jewel beetle

water scorpion

firefly

cricket

rhinoceros beetle

cricket

carabid beetle

diving beetle

cicada

mole cricket

long-horned beetle

cicada

cockroach

water strider

scorpion

katydid

locust

cockroach

cricket

pill bug

centipede

water scorpion

firefly

fly

bee

scorpion

stick insect

fly

pill bug

butterfly

moth

locust

mole cricket

jewel beetle

ladybug

dragonfly

cricket

spider

26 Birds of a Feather Stay Together (Matching 30)

Perfect	within 1 minute, 30 seconds
Excellent	within 2 minutes, 30 seconds
Super	within 3 minutes, 30 seconds
Great	within 4 minutes, 30 seconds
Very good	within 5 minutes, 30 seconds
Good	within 7 minutes
Fair	within 9 minutes
Satisfactory	within 11 minutes
Keep Trying	more than 11 minutes

DATE NAME TIME

Circle the matching birds.

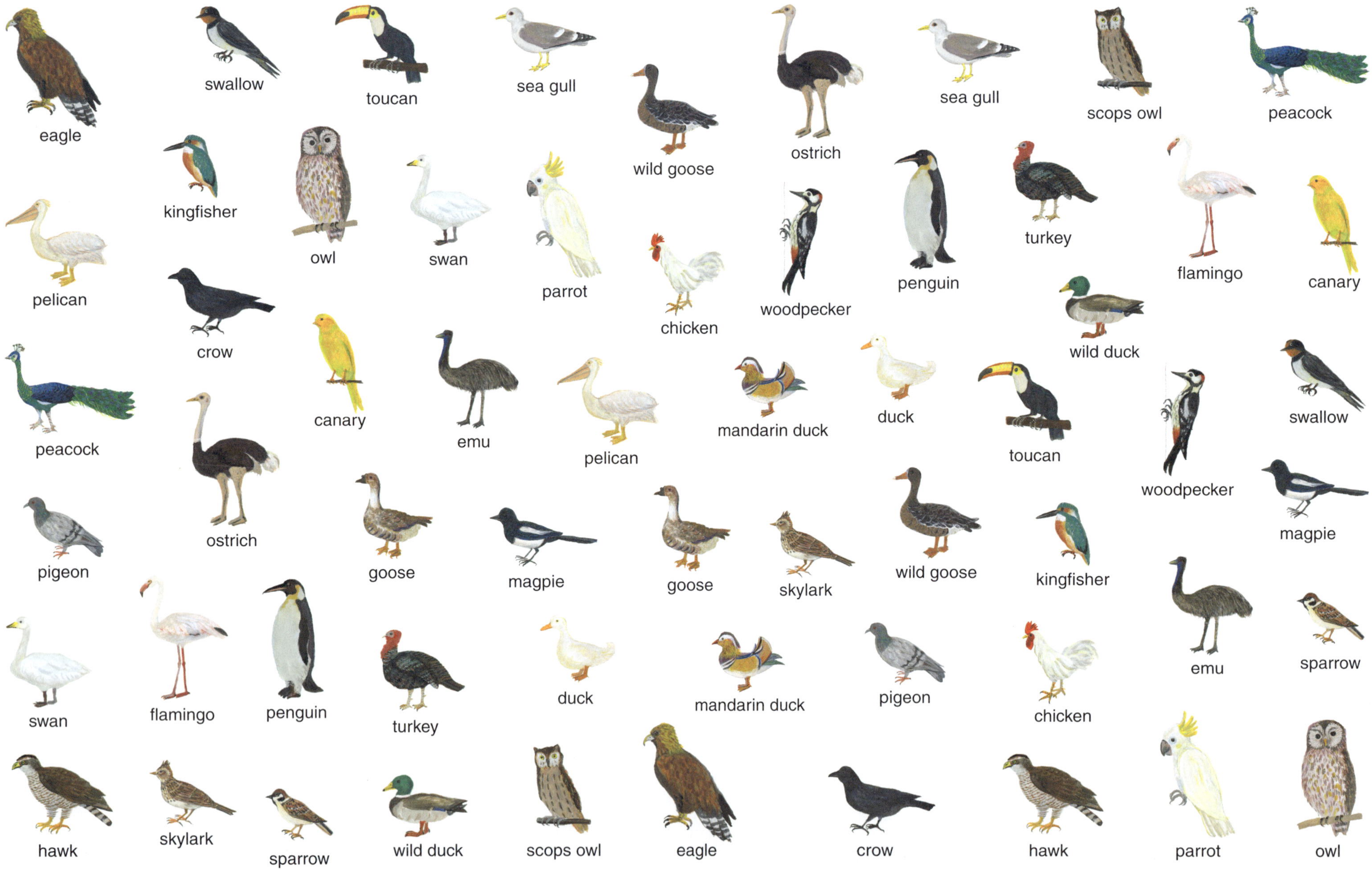
eagle
swallow
toucan
sea gull
wild goose
ostrich
sea gull
scops owl
peacock
kingfisher
owl
swan
parrot
chicken
woodpecker
penguin
turkey
flamingo
canary
pelican
crow
wild duck
peacock
canary
emu
pelican
mandarin duck
duck
toucan
woodpecker
swallow
ostrich
pigeon
goose
magpie
goose
skylark
wild goose
kingfisher
magpie
swan
flamingo
penguin
turkey
duck
mandarin duck
pigeon
chicken
emu
sparrow
hawk
skylark
sparrow
wild duck
scops owl
eagle
crow
hawk
parrot
owl

Circle the matching animals.

DATE   NAME   TIME

elephant
squirrel
chimpanzee
leopard
cheetah
chimpanzee
rhinoceros
gorilla
giraffe
crocodile
goat
panda
seal
rabbit
bottlenose dolphin
horse
guinea pig
zebra
kangaroo
fox
mouse
bear
gorilla
cow
deer
panda
fox
squirrel
tiger
frog
mole
frog
lion
hippopotamus
tortoise
cow
bottlenose dolphin
pig
kangaroo
koala
tortoise
cheetah
rhinoceros
tiger
deer
mole
bear
wild boar
mouse
seal
elephant
rabbit
hippopotamus
wild boar
zebra
giraffe
crocodile
horse
goat
lion
pig
koala
leopard
guinea pig

Perfect within 1 minute, 30 seconds	**Great** within 4 minutes, 30 seconds	**Fair** within 9 minutes
Excellent within 2 minutes, 30 seconds	**Very good** within 5 minutes, 30 seconds	**Satisfactory** within 11 minutes
Super within 3 minutes, 30 seconds	**Good** within 7 minutes	**Keep Trying** more than 11 minutes

DATE   NAME   TIME

manta ray · arowana · scorpion fish · piranha · sole · cod fish · swordfish · hammerhead shark

anglerfish · bonito · flying fish · carp · tuna · black bass · anglerfish

sea horse · black bass · salmon · ray · sea bream · eel · loach · blowfish

porcupine fish · tuna · goldfish · scorpion fish · manta ray · shark

shark · coelacanth · flatfish · anchovy · goldfish · catfish · angelfish

angelfish · ray · cutlassfish · blowfish · jack · flatfish · sunfish

sunfish · catfish · loach · carp · porcupine fish · jack

swordfish · cod fish · sea bream · sea horse · flying fish · cutlassfish · anchovy

sole · hammerhead shark · eel · bonito · arowana · salmon · piranha · coelacanth

29 At the Farmer's Market (Matching 32)

Perfect within 1 minute, 30 seconds	**Great** within 4 minutes, 30 seconds	**Fair** within 9 minutes
Excellent within 2 minutes, 30 seconds	**Very good** within 5 minutes, 30 seconds	**Satisfactory** within 11 minutes
Super within 3 minutes, 30 seconds	**Good** within 7 minutes	**Keep Trying** more than 11 minutes

DATE NAME TIME

Circle the matching produce.

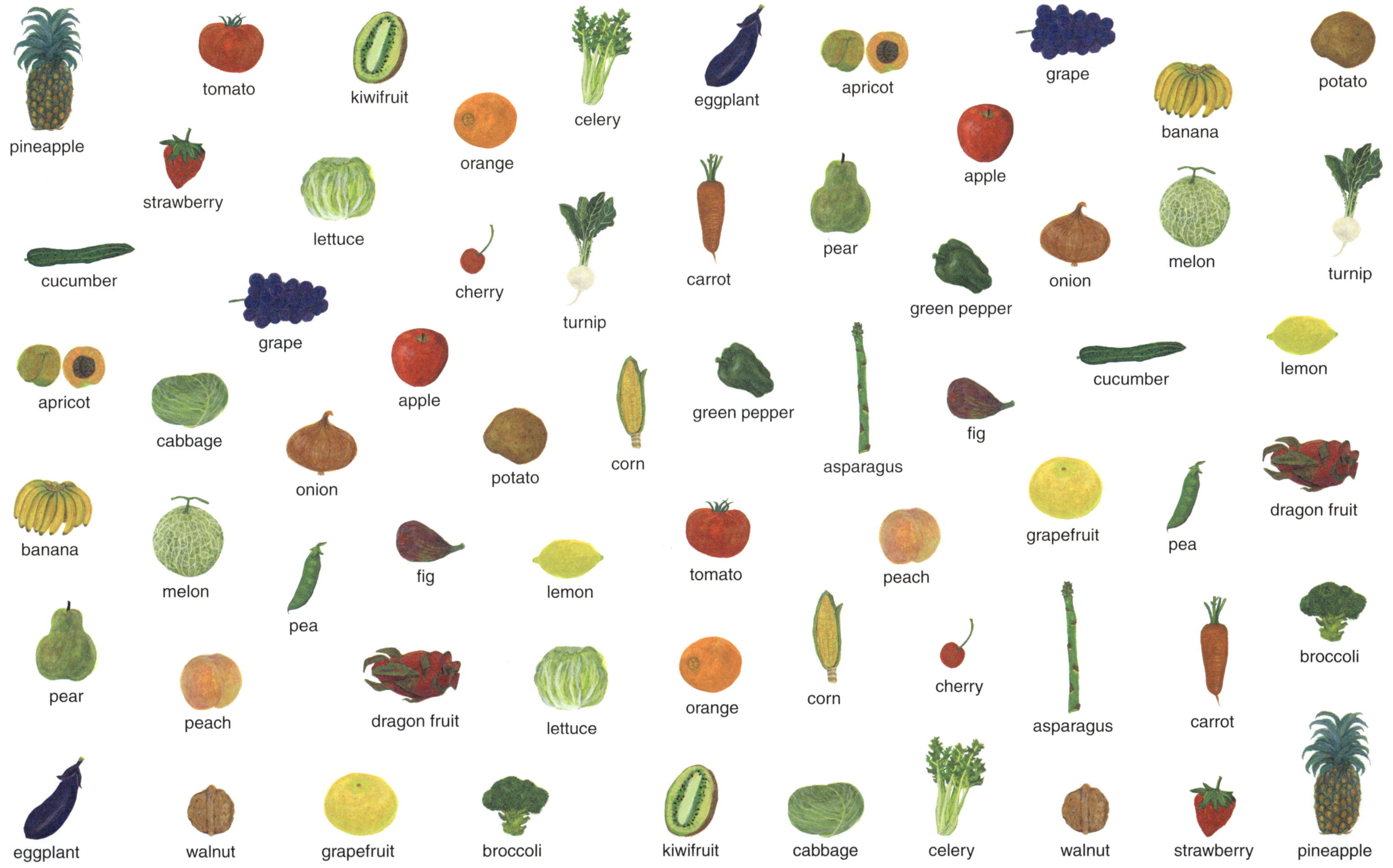
pineapple
tomato
kiwifruit
orange
celery
eggplant
apricot
grape
banana
potato
strawberry
lettuce
apple
pear
cucumber
cherry
turnip
carrot
green pepper
onion
melon
turnip
grape
apricot
apple
cabbage
green pepper
cucumber
lemon
onion
potato
corn
asparagus
fig
banana
melon
fig
lemon
tomato
peach
grapefruit
pea
dragon fruit
pea
pear
peach
dragon fruit
lettuce
orange
corn
cherry
asparagus
carrot
broccoli
eggplant
walnut
grapefruit
broccoli
kiwifruit
cabbage
celery
walnut
strawberry
pineapple

■ Circle the matching flowers.

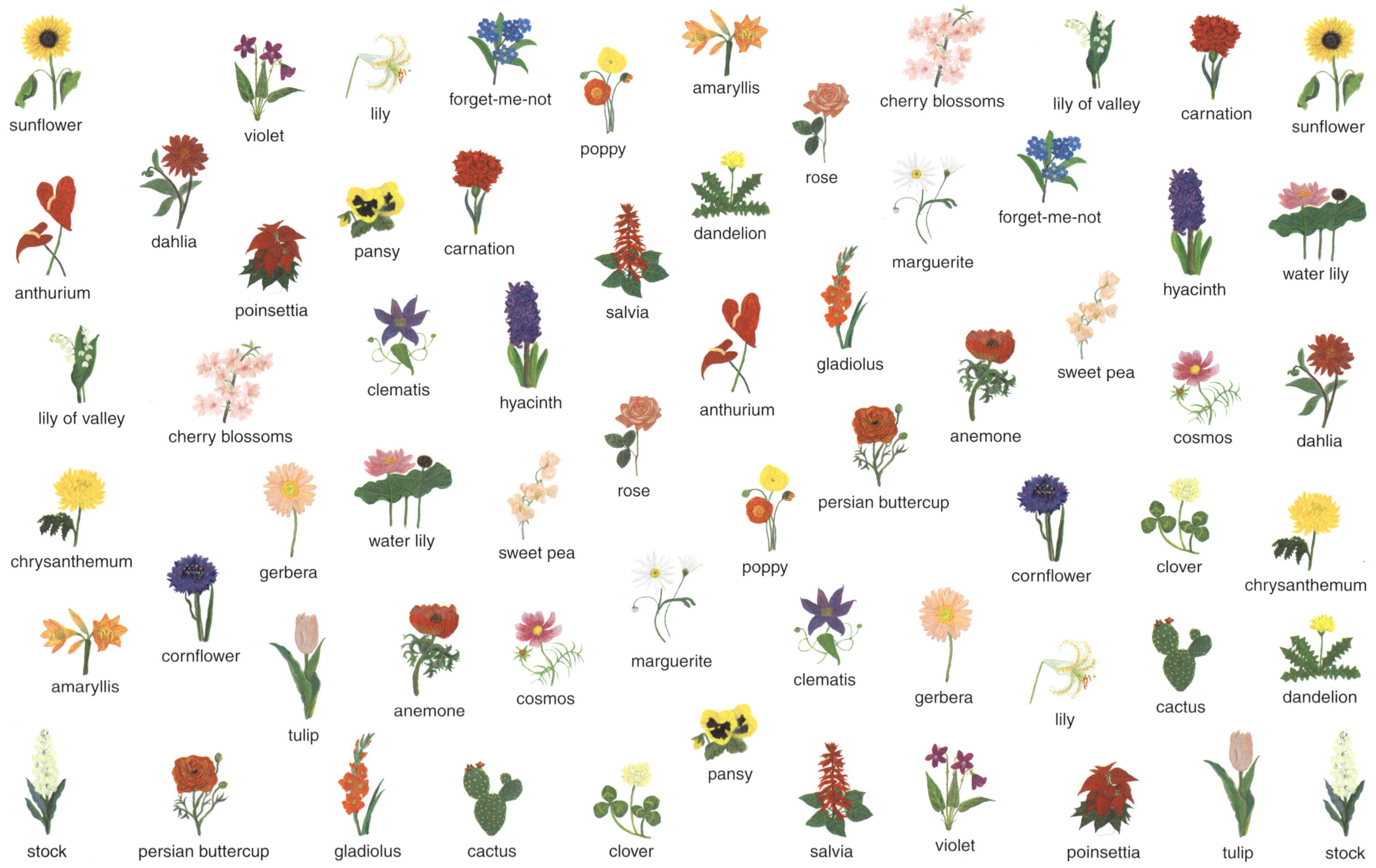

 **Perfect** within 1 minute, 30 seconds	**Great** within 4 minutes, 30 seconds	**Fair** within 9 minutes
Excellent within 2 minutes, 30 seconds	**Very good** within 5 minutes, 30 seconds	**Satisfactory** within 11 minutes
Super within 3 minutes, 30 seconds	**Good** within 7 minutes	**Keep Trying** more than 11 minutes

DATE   NAME   TIME

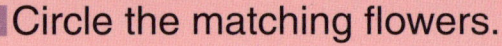

sunflower

violet

lily

forget-me-not

amaryllis

poppy

cherry blossoms

lily of valley

carnation

sunflower

dahlia

anthurium

pansy

carnation

rose

dandelion

forget-me-not

marguerite

hyacinth

water lily

poinsettia

salvia

clematis

hyacinth

anthurium

gladiolus

sweet pea

lily of valley

cherry blossoms

rose

anemone

cosmos

dahlia

chrysanthemum

water lily

sweet pea

persian buttercup

cornflower

clover

chrysanthemum

gerbera

rose

poppy

amaryllis

cornflower

marguerite

clematis

gerbera

lily

cactus

dandelion

tulip

anemone

cosmos

pansy

stock

persian buttercup

gladiolus

cactus

clover

salvia

violet

poinsettia

tulip

stock

Circle the matching insects.

🚀 **Perfect** within 1 minute, 30 seconds	🚌 **Great** within 4 minutes, 30 seconds	🚲 **Fair** within 9 minutes	
✈️ **Excellent** within 2 minutes, 30 seconds	🚗 **Very good** within 5 minutes, 30 seconds	🛴 **Satisfactory** within 11 minutes	
🚁 **Super** within 3 minutes, 30 seconds	🐎 **Good** within 7 minutes	🏃 **Keep Trying** more than 11 minutes	

DATE   NAME   TIME

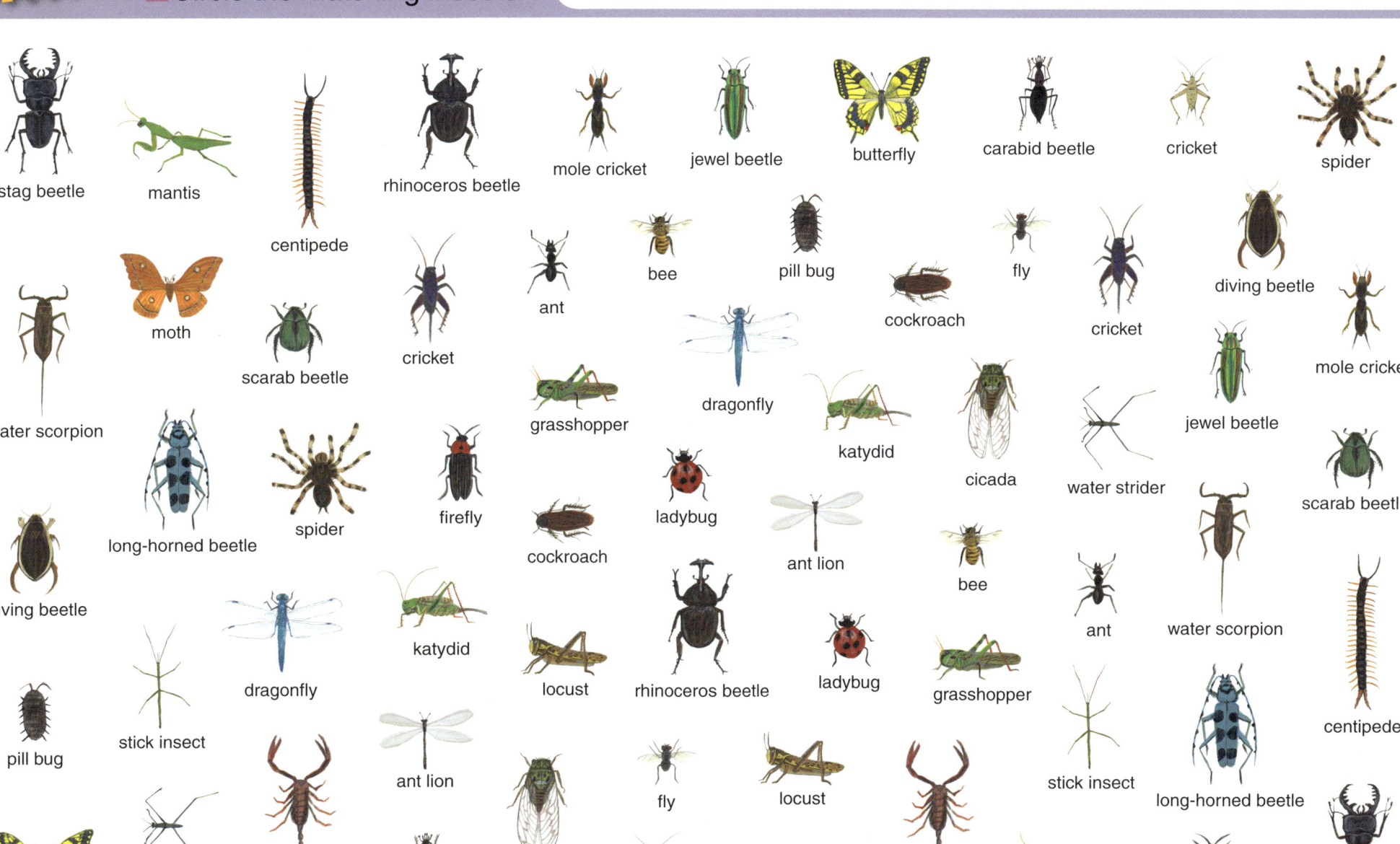

stag beetle · mantis · centipede · rhinoceros beetle · mole cricket · jewel beetle · butterfly · carabid beetle · cricket · spider

moth · scarab beetle · cricket · ant · bee · pill bug · cockroach · fly · cricket · diving beetle

water scorpion · long-horned beetle · spider · firefly · grasshopper · dragonfly · katydid · cicada · water strider · jewel beetle · mole cricket

diving beetle · dragonfly · katydid · cockroach · ladybug · ant lion · bee · ant · water scorpion · scarab beetle

pill bug · stick insect · ant lion · locust · rhinoceros beetle · ladybug · grasshopper · stick insect · long-horned beetle · centipede

butterfly · water strider · scorpion · carabid beetle · cicada · cricket · fly · locust · scorpion · moth · mantis · firefly · stag beetle

32 Birds of a Feather Stay Together (Matching 32)

Perfect within 1 minute, 30 seconds
Excellent within 2 minutes, 30 seconds
Super within 3 minutes, 30 seconds
Great within 4 minutes, 30 seconds
Very good within 5 minutes, 30 seconds
Good within 7 minutes
Fair within 9 minutes
Satisfactory within 11 minutes
Keep Trying more than 11 minutes

DATE NAME TIME

Circle the matching birds.

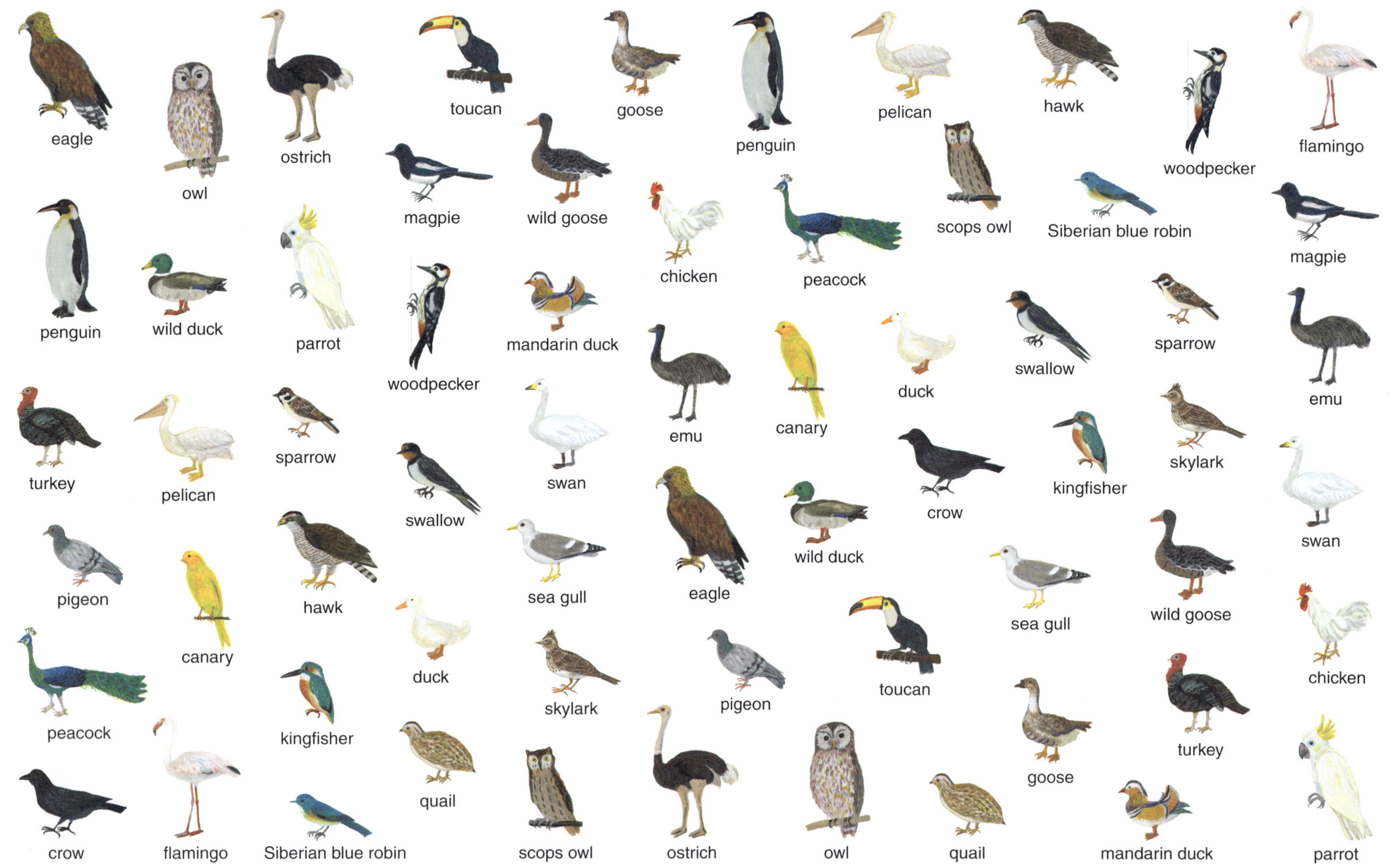

eagle
owl
ostrich
toucan
goose
penguin
pelican
hawk
woodpecker
flamingo
magpie
wild goose
chicken
peacock
scops owl
Siberian blue robin
magpie
penguin
wild duck
parrot
woodpecker
mandarin duck
emu
canary
duck
swallow
sparrow
emu
turkey
pelican
sparrow
swallow
swan
eagle
wild duck
crow
kingfisher
skylark
swan
pigeon
canary
hawk
sea gull
sea gull
wild goose
duck
skylark
pigeon
toucan
chicken
peacock
kingfisher
quail
goose
turkey
crow
flamingo
Siberian blue robin
scops owl
ostrich
owl
quail
mandarin duck
parrot

Exploring the Zoo

(Matching 34)

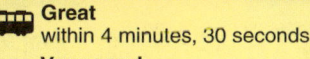
DATE   NAME   TIME

■ Circle the matching animals.

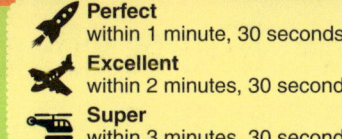

elephant

rhinoceros

leopard

hippopotamus

tiger

bear

lion

giraffe

chimpanzee

frog

koala

tortoise

bottlenose dolphin

mole

zebra

rabbit

wild boar

polar bear

squirrel

horse

guinea pig

cow

zebra

hamster

kangaroo

horse

gorilla

cheetah

crocodile

bottlenose dolphin

mole

rabbit

mouse

fox

panda

polar bear

hamster

koala

tiger

bear

cheetah

cow

pig

crocodile

hippopotamus

deer

pig

fox

giraffe

goat

seal

frog

kangaroo

goat

mouse

chimpanzee

wild boar

deer

seal

squirrel

tortoise

panda

lion

guinea pig

elephant

leopard

gorilla

rhinoceros

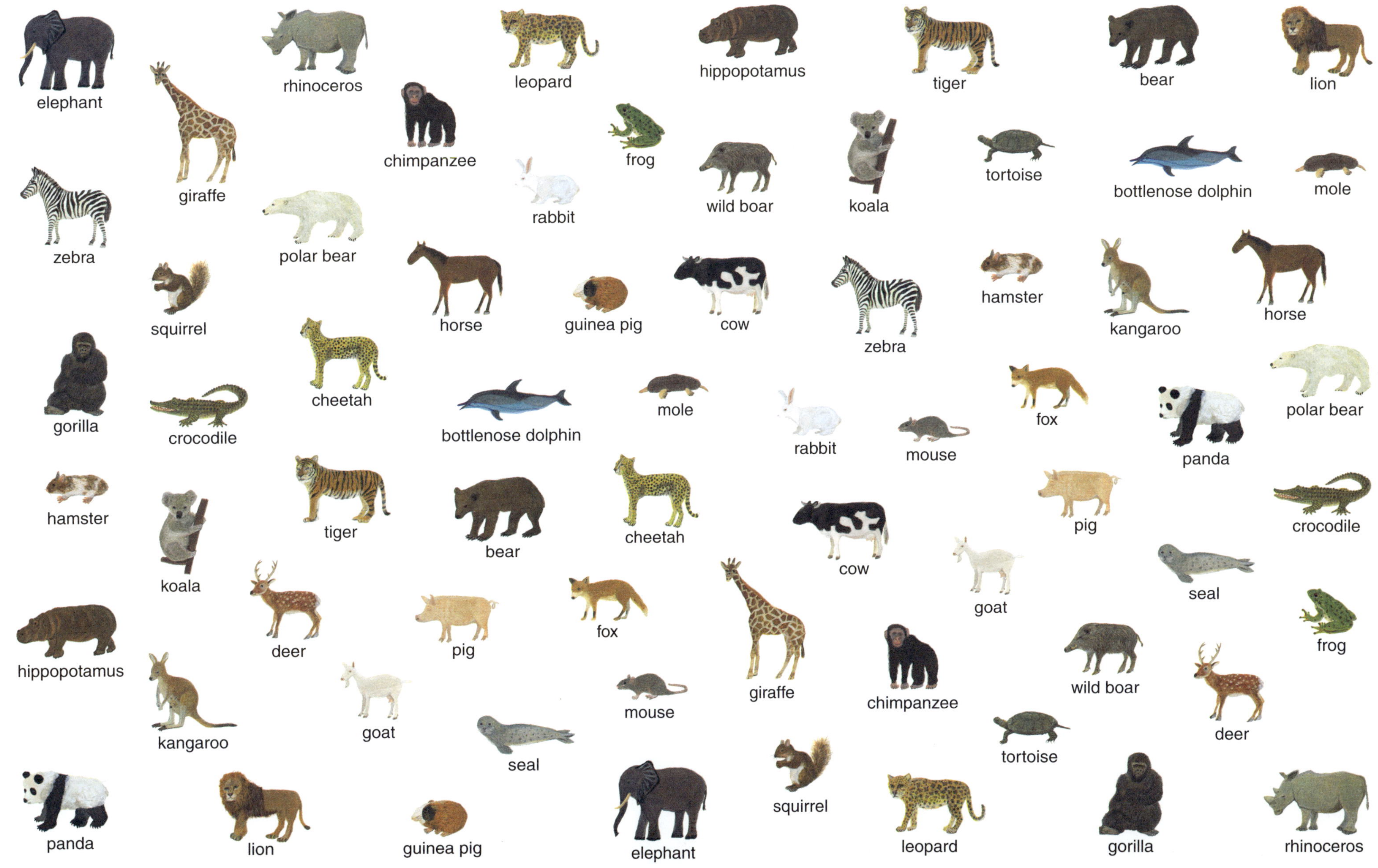

Circle the matching fish.

	Perfect within 1 minute, 30 seconds		Great within 4 minutes, 30 seconds		Fair within 9 minutes
	Excellent within 2 minutes, 30 seconds		Very good within 5 minutes, 30 seconds		Satisfactory within 11 minutes
	Super within 3 minutes, 30 seconds		Good within 7 minutes		Keep Trying more than 11 minutes

DATE   NAME   TIME

humphead wrasse · porcupine fish · cutlassfish · eel · manta ray · arowana · piranha

sea horse · arowana · carp · piranha · flying fish · porcupine fish · scorpion fish

scorpion fish · ray · salmon · bonito · coelacanth · rainbow trout · cutlassfish

anglerfish · flatfish · catfish · tuna · jack · swordfish · hammerhead shark

sea horse · angelfish · sea bream · carp · tuna · shark

sunfish · shark · anglerfish · cod fish · flying fish

hammerhead shark · blowfish · eel · goldfish · catfish

sole · swordfish · black bass · rainbow trout · anchovy · bonito · blowfish

coelacanth · cod fish · loach · anchovy · sea bream · black bass · salmon · angelfish

manta ray · goldfish · sole · ray · sunfish · flatfish · loach · jack · humphead wrasse

35 At the Farmer's Market (Matching 34)

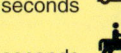

Perfect within 1 minute, 30 seconds
Excellent within 2 minutes, 30 seconds
Super within 3 minutes, 30 seconds
Great within 4 minutes, 30 seconds
Very good within 5 minutes, 30 seconds
Good within 7 minutes
Fair within 9 minutes
Satisfactory within 11 minutes
Keep Trying more than 11 minutes

Circle the matching produce.

DATE NAME TIME

pea
onion
pineapple
cauliflower
orange
kiwifruit
turnip
apricot
tomato
asparagus
corn
lettuce
green pepper
eggplant
celery
fig
lettuce
potato
carrot
apple
banana
eggplant
grape
cabbage
carrot
peach
tomato
pea
onion
cherry
cucumber
peach
lemon
strawberry
grapefruit
asparagus
dragon fruit
cucumber
cherry
grapefruit
apple
melon
corn
cabbage
pear
melon
turnip
banana
durian
orange
broccoli
walnut
grape
dragon fruit
apricot
broccoli
walnut
kiwifruit
strawberry
celery
potato
cauliflower
fig
green pepper
pineapple
pear
durian
lemon

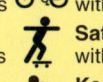

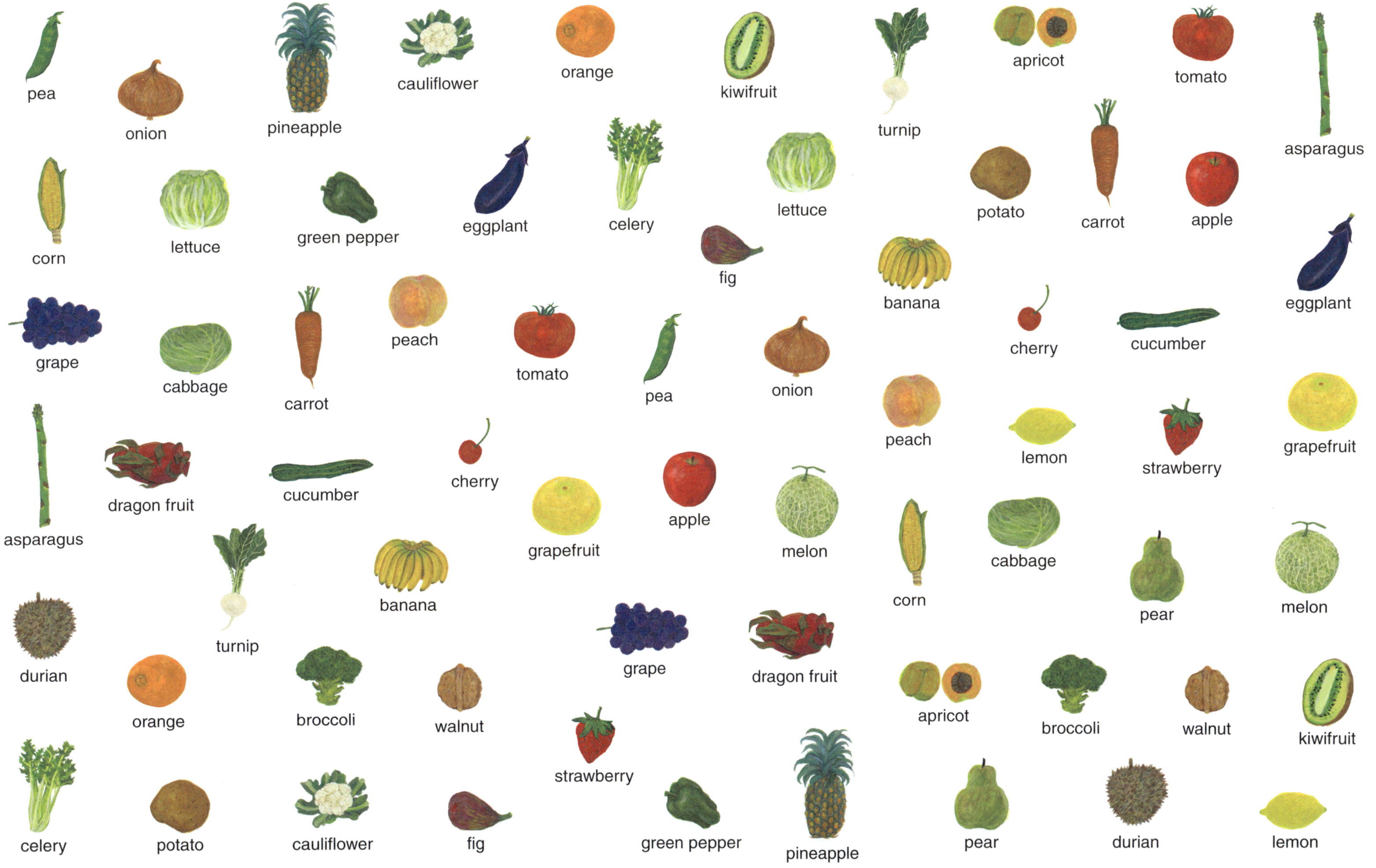

■ Circle the matching flowers.

DATE   NAME   TIME

pansy, hyacinth, cherry blossoms, clematis, lily of valley, magnolia, anthurium, dandelion, marguerite, cornflower, forget-me-not, salvia, lily, chrysanthemum, gladiolus, stock, clover, cosmos, forget-me-not, water lily, tulip, dahlia, sweet pea, gerbera, carnation, peach, poinsettia, peach, gerbera, cactus, water lily, poinsettia, anemone, rose, violet, dahlia, rose, carnation, sunflower, poppy, clover, cosmos, stock, magnolia, hyacinth, tulip, amaryllis, violet, gladiolus, anthurium, cornflower, marguerite, amaryllis, sunflower, cactus, chrysanthemum, persian buttercup, cherry blossoms, poppy, anemone, dandelion, persian buttercup, pansy, clematis, lily, sweet pea, salvia, lily of valley

Circle the matching insects.

DATE   NAME   TIME

giant water bug

diving beetle

horsefly

katydid

ladybug

stag beetle

firefly

ant

cockroach

water scorpion

cicada

ant

bee

grasshopper

katydid

mole cricket

centipede

scarab beetle

butterfly

water strider

carabid beetle

scarab beetle

water scorpion

dragonfly

scorpion

pill bug

spider

long-horned beetle

mole cricket

pill bug

jewel beetle

grasshopper

dragonfly

cockroach

carabid beetle

ladybug

locust

stag beetle

spider

rhinoceros beetle

cricket

moth

locust

cicada

ant lion

cricket

stick insect

firefly

stick insect

cricket

fly

long-horned beetle

butterfly

horsefly

water strider

mantis

cricket

moth

centipede

mantis

scorpion

ant lion

giant water bug

diving beetle

fly

jewel beetle

bee

rhinoceros beetle

Birds of a Feather Stay Together (Matching 34)

	Perfect within 1 minute, 30 seconds		Great within 4 minutes, 30 seconds		Fair within 9 minutes
	Excellent within 2 minutes, 30 seconds		Very good within 5 minutes, 30 seconds		Satisfactory within 11 minutes
	Super within 3 minutes, 30 seconds		Good within 7 minutes		Keep Trying more than 11 minutes

DATE　　　　NAME　　　　TIME

■ Circle the matching birds.

■ Circle the matching animals.

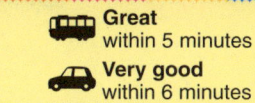
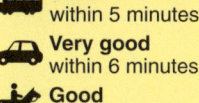
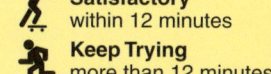
DATE   NAME   TIME

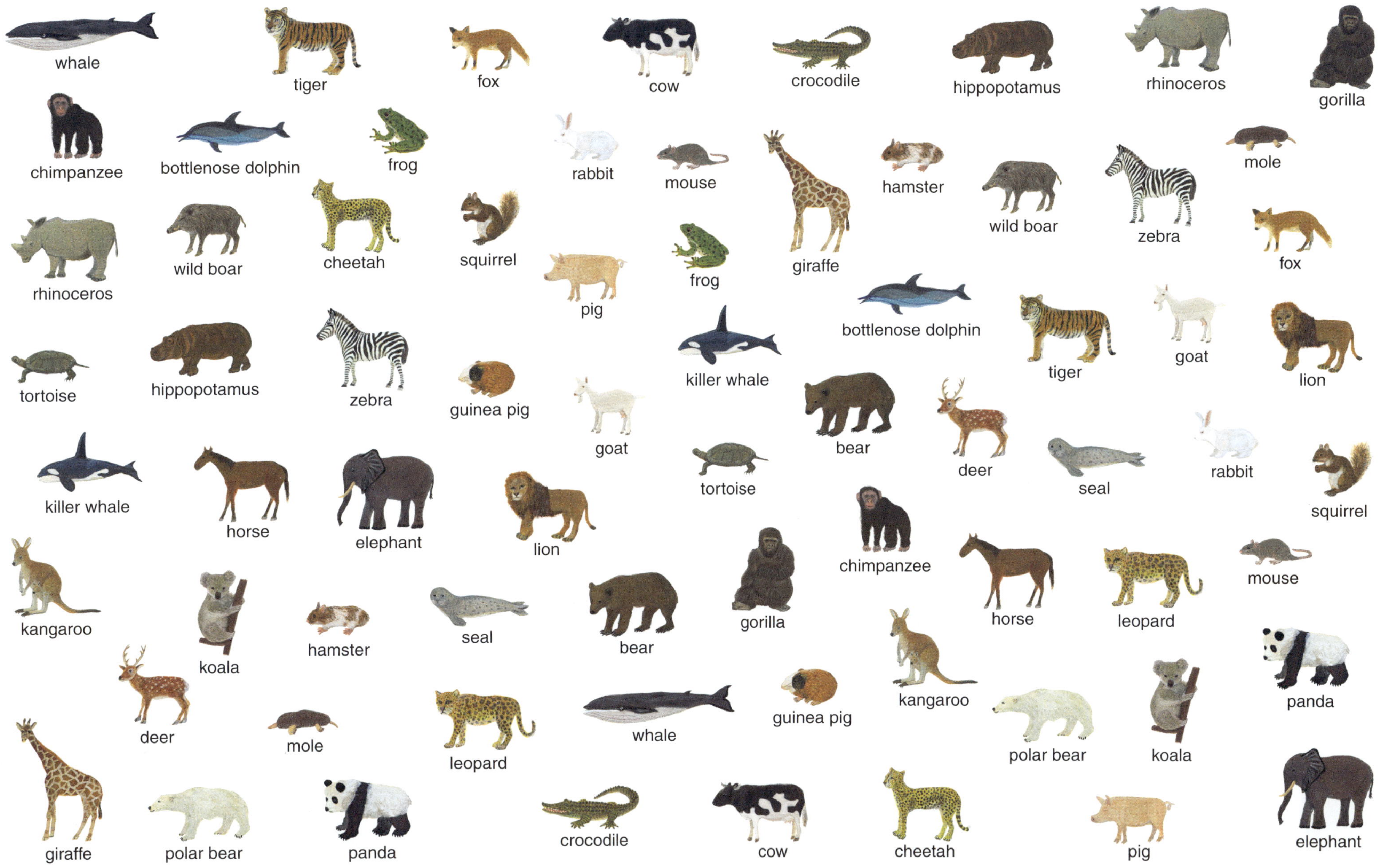

whale

tiger

fox

cow

crocodile

hippopotamus

rhinoceros

gorilla

chimpanzee

bottlenose dolphin

frog

rabbit

mouse

hamster

wild boar

zebra

mole

rhinoceros

wild boar

cheetah

squirrel

pig

frog

giraffe

wild boar

zebra

fox

tortoise

hippopotamus

zebra

guinea pig

goat

killer whale

bottlenose dolphin

tiger

goat

lion

killer whale

horse

elephant

lion

tortoise

bear

deer

seal

rabbit

squirrel

kangaroo

koala

hamster

seal

bear

gorilla

chimpanzee

horse

leopard

mouse

deer

mole

leopard

whale

guinea pig

kangaroo

polar bear

koala

panda

giraffe

polar bear

panda

crocodile

cow

cheetah

pig

elephant

Circle the matching fish.

DATE   NAME   TIME

manta ray, scorpion fish, moray, rainbow trout, salmon, cutlassfish, blowfish, tuna, hammerhead shark

angelfish, anglerfish, piranha, swordfish, catfish, cod fish, black bass, flatfish

sole, arowana, flying fish, humphead wrasse, porcupine fish, sunfish

coelacanth, shark, tuna, bonito, carp, jack, anchovy, herring, ray

humphead wrasse, porcupine fish, jack, anchovy, ray, anglerfish, goldfish, eel, carp, sea horse, angelfish

cod fish, flatfish, herring, sea bream, piranha, bonito, rainbow trout, flying fish, loach, catfish

blowfish, black bass, sunfish, sea horse, eel, scorpion fish, salmon, swordfish, coelacanth, sea bream

cutlassfish, hammerhead shark, goldfish, loach, manta ray, moray, shark, arowana, sole

41 At the Farmer's Market (Matching 36)

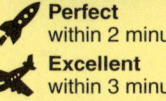

Perfect within 2 minutes
Excellent within 3 minutes
Super within 4 minutes
Great within 5 minutes
Very good within 6 minutes
Good within 8 minutes
Fair within 10 minutes
Satisfactory within 12 minutes
Keep Trying more than 12 minutes

DATE NAME TIME

Circle the matching produce.

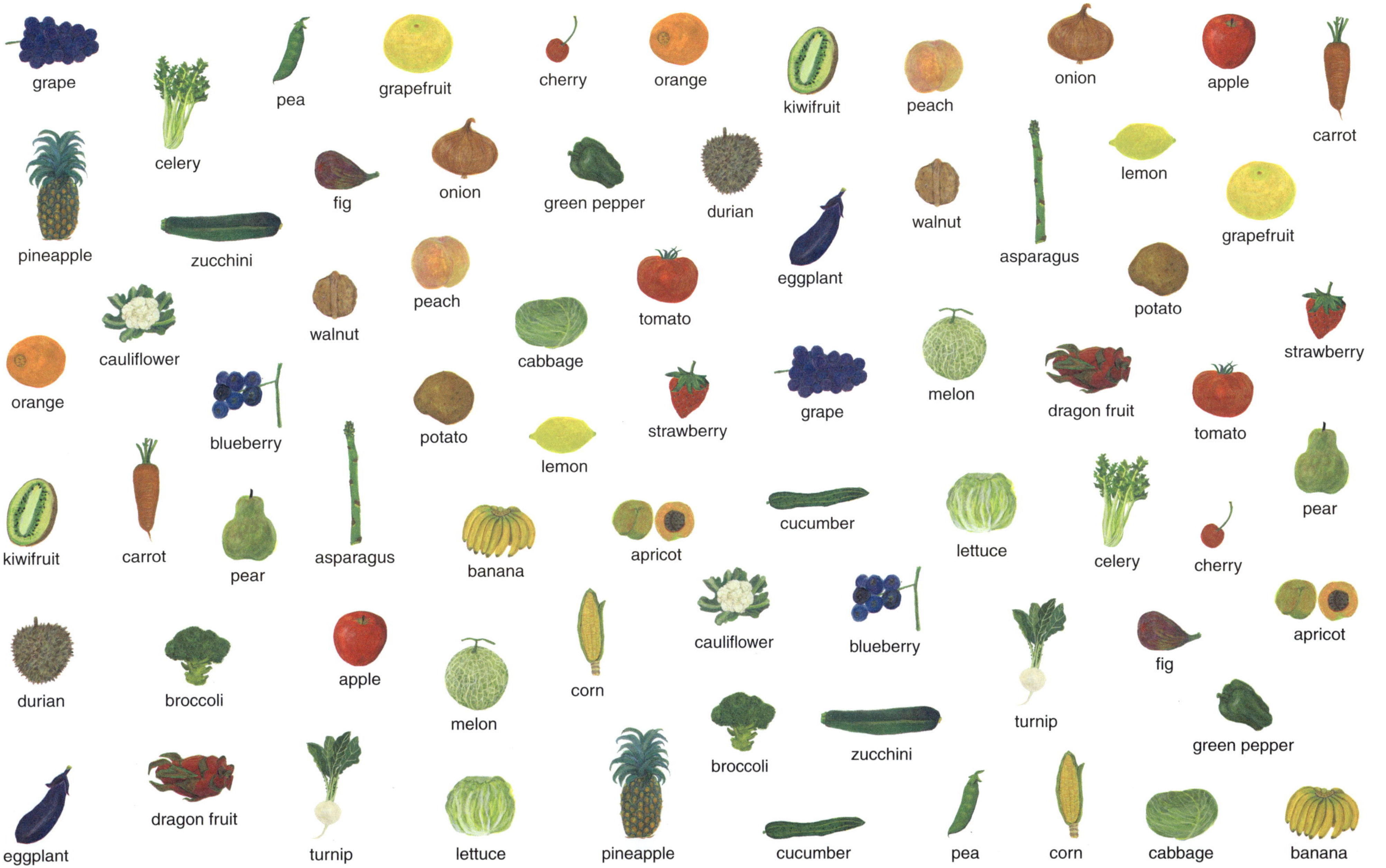

grape
pea
grapefruit
cherry
orange
kiwifruit
peach
onion
apple
carrot
celery
pineapple
fig
onion
green pepper
durian
walnut
lemon
asparagus
grapefruit
zucchini
eggplant
peach
walnut
tomato
potato
cauliflower
cabbage
strawberry
melon
orange
blueberry
grape
dragon fruit
tomato
potato
strawberry
lemon
kiwifruit
carrot
pear
asparagus
banana
apricot
cucumber
lettuce
celery
cherry
pear
cauliflower
blueberry
apricot
durian
broccoli
apple
corn
melon
fig
turnip
broccoli
zucchini
green pepper
eggplant
dragon fruit
turnip
lettuce
pineapple
cucumber
pea
corn
cabbage
banana

Picking Flowers
(Matching 36)

■ Circle the matching flowers.

DATE   NAME   TIME

cherry blossoms clematis forget-me-not persian buttercup marguerite rose poinsettia calla salvia dahlia hyacinth

stock gerbera salvia sunflower tulip violet cherry blossoms poppy clematis amaryllis sunflower rose tulip

poinsettia amaryllis dahlia chrysanthemum clover carnation anthurium cornflower water lily marguerite anemone lily

cornflower magnolia

hyacinth cactus lily peach gladiolus iris gerbera lily of valley gladiolus persian buttercup cosmos chrysanthemum

carnation sweet pea water lily pansy dandelion anemone forget-me-not cactus clover dandelion violet

iris calla anthurium poppy cosmos stock sweet pea pansy peach lily of valley magnolia

43 Catch the Bug

(Matching 36)

Circle the matching insects.

Perfect within 2 minutes	**Great** within 5 minutes	**Fair** within 10 minutes
Excellent within 3 minutes	**Very good** within 6 minutes	**Satisfactory** within 12 minutes
Super within 4 minutes	**Good** within 8 minutes	**Keep Trying** more than 12 minutes

DATE   NAME   TIME

rhinoceros beetle

long-horned beetle

scarab beetle

ladybug

ant

bee

mantis

water scorpion

ant

spider

centipede

firefly

moth

cicada

jewel beetle

moth

firefly

water scorpion

stick insect

scorpion

jewel beetle

cockroach

bee

drone beetle

diving beetle

stag beetle

ladybug

fly

mole cricket

stick insect

pill bug

cricket

locust

cicada

katydid

mole cricket

long-horned beetle

cricket

drone beetle

dragonfly

grasshopper

pill bug

water strider

spider

grasshopper

giant water bug

katydid

scorpion

tiger beetle

locust

ant lion

centipede

butterfly

tiger beetle

dragonfly

ant lion

cricket

horsefly

diving beetle

cricket

fly

carabid beetle

stag beetle

mantis

horsefly

carabid beetle

cockroach

rhinoceros beetle

giant water bug

butterfly

scarab beetle

water strider

Birds of a Feather Stay Together (Matching 36)

Circle the matching birds.

🚀 **Perfect** within 2 minutes	🚌 **Great** within 5 minutes	🚲 **Fair** within 10 minutes
✈️ **Excellent** within 3 minutes	🚗 **Very good** within 6 minutes	🛹 **Satisfactory** within 12 minutes
🚁 **Super** within 4 minutes	🐴 **Good** within 8 minutes	🏋️ **Keep Trying** more than 12 minutes

DATE   NAME   TIME

eagle

duck

penguin

quail

cuckoo

woodpecker

peacock

sparrow

hawk

owl

sea gull

kingfisher

ostrich

turkey

goose

albatross

condor

emu

quail

toucan

crow

condor

emu

swallow

parrot

swallow

hummingbird

sea gull

parrot

ostrich

wild duck

goose

Siberian blue robin

canary

mandarin duck

chicken

hummingbird

canary

scops owl

flamingo

cuckoo

kingfisher

woodpecker

peacock

pigeon

swan

owl

swan

flamingo

wild duck

pelican

sparrow

hawk

magpie

pelican

albatross

duck

toucan

skylark

turkey

chicken

scops owl

wild goose

flamingo

skylark

eagle

penguin

mandarin duck

pigeon

magpie

wild goose

Siberian blue robin

crow

Exploring the Zoo
(Matching 38)

■ Circle the matching animals.

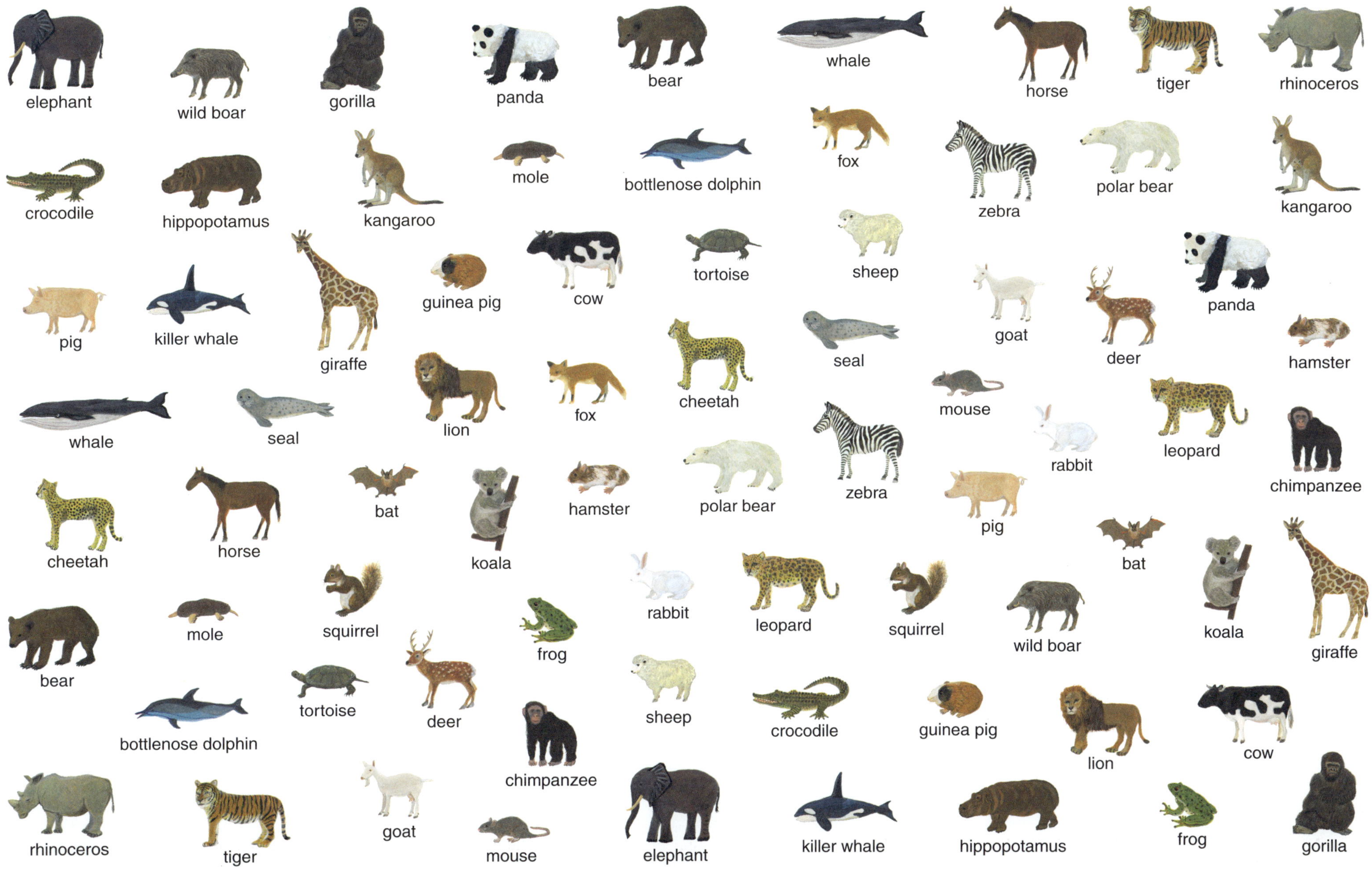

DATE   NAME   TIME

elephant   wild boar   gorilla   panda   bear   whale   horse   tiger   rhinoceros

crocodile   hippopotamus   kangaroo   mole   bottlenose dolphin   fox   zebra   polar bear   kangaroo

pig   killer whale   giraffe   guinea pig   cow   tortoise   sheep   goat   deer   panda   hamster

whale   seal   lion   fox   cheetah   seal   mouse   rabbit   leopard   chimpanzee

cheetah   horse   bat   koala   hamster   polar bear   zebra   pig   bat   koala   giraffe

bear   mole   squirrel   deer   frog   rabbit   leopard   squirrel   wild boar   koala

bottlenose dolphin   tortoise   sheep   crocodile   guinea pig   lion   cow

chimpanzee

rhinoceros   tiger   goat   mouse   elephant   killer whale   hippopotamus   frog   gorilla

46 Dive into the Water
(Matching 38)

■ Circle the matching fish.

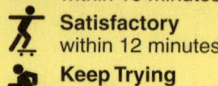

humphead wrasse

flatfish

anchovy

bonito

manta ray

scorpion fish

coelacanth

sea horse

anglerfish

ray

anglerfish

porcupine fish

sea bream

herring

carp

piranha

salmon

herring

yellow tail

cod fish

flying fish

sole

parrot fish

black bass

porcupine fish

manta ray

cutlassfish

sea horse

tuna

scorpion fish

anchovy

sunfish

arowana

blowfish

eel

arowana

carp

swordfish

salmon

black bass

jack

shark

rainbow trout

jack

blowfish

angelfish

moray

catfish

swordfish

flying fish

loach

parrot fish

piranha

yellow tail

hammerhead shark

goldfish

rainbow trout

cutlassfish

goldfish

sunfish

cod fish

ray

tuna

coelacanth

angelfish

catfish

flatfish

loach

sole

eel

shark

moray

humphead wrasse

bonito

hammerhead shark

sea bream

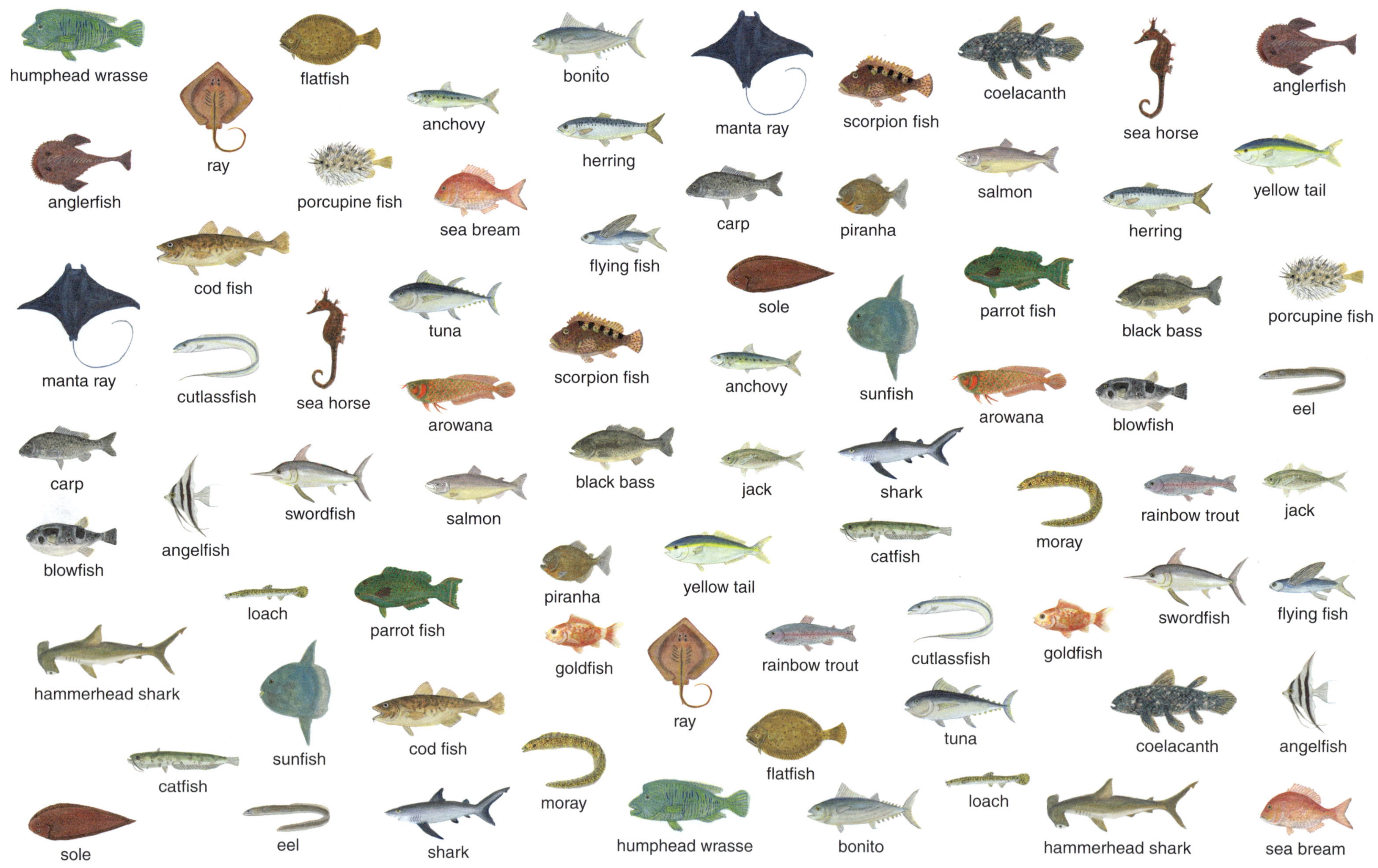

■ Circle the matching produce.

DATE   NAME   TIME

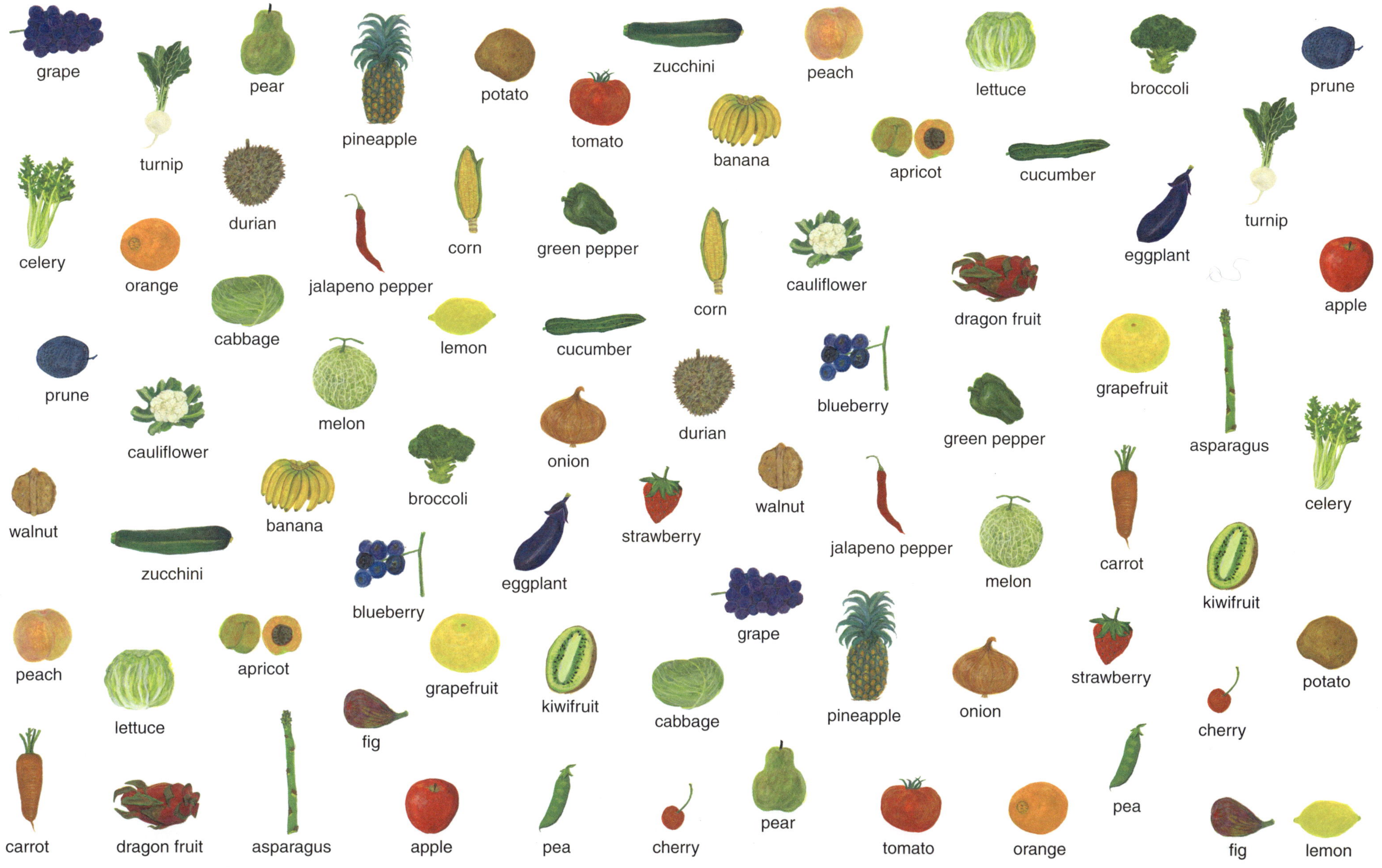

grape

pear

pineapple

potato

tomato

zucchini

peach

lettuce

broccoli

prune

turnip

banana

apricot

cucumber

durian

corn

green pepper

turnip

celery

orange

jalapeno pepper

cauliflower

corn

eggplant

apple

cabbage

lemon

cucumber

dragon fruit

grapefruit

prune

melon

durian

blueberry

green pepper

asparagus

cauliflower

onion

walnut

jalapeno pepper

melon

celery

walnut

banana

broccoli

strawberry

carrot

zucchini

eggplant

kiwifruit

blueberry

grape

strawberry

peach

grapefruit

pineapple

potato

apricot

kiwifruit

onion

lettuce

cabbage

cherry

fig

carrot

dragon fruit

asparagus

apple

pea

cherry

pear

tomato

orange

pea

fig

lemon

■ Circle the matching flowers.

	Perfect within 2 minutes		Great within 5 minutes		Fair within 10 minutes
Excellent within 3 minutes		Very good within 6 minutes		Satisfactory within 12 minutes
Super within 4 minutes		Good within 8 minutes		Keep Trying more than 12 minutes

DATE   NAME   TIME

violet, forget-me-not, anthurium, iris, pansy, stock, water lily, gerbera, cornflower, forget-me-not, sweet pea, clematis, gladiolus, cattleya, marguerite, water lily, rose, bellflower, anemone, cactus, rose, amaryllis, gladiolus, calla, hyacinth, cherry blossoms, salvia, cornflower, lily of valley, clematis, persian buttercup, iris, cattleya, marguerite, carnation, anthurium, stock, amaryllis, sunflower, cactus, tulip, cosmos, sunflower, pansy, cosmos, carnation, dandelion, gerbera, magnolia, salvia, peach, sweet pea, dahlia, calla, peach, dandelion, poppy, lily of valley, lily, dahlia, magnolia, bellflower, chrysanthemum, chrysanthemum, poinsettia, persian buttercup, lily, anemone, poppy, hyacinth, clover, poinsettia, cherry blossoms, tulip, violet, clover

49 Catch the Bug
(Matching 38)

Circle the matching insects.

🚀 **Perfect** within 2 minutes	🚌 **Great** within 5 minutes	🚴 **Fair** within 10 minutes
✈️ **Excellent** within 3 minutes	🚗 **Very good** within 6 minutes	⛸️ **Satisfactory** within 12 minutes
🚁 **Super** within 4 minutes	🐴 **Good** within 8 minutes	🤸 **Keep Trying** more than 12 minutes

DATE   NAME   TIME

rhinoceros beetle   ladybug   giant water bug   centipede   katydid   butterfly   dragonfly   spider   pill bug   cockroach   long-horned beetle

scarab beetle   cricket   grasshopper   cricket   stick insect

butterfly   stag beetle   mole cricket   mantis   drone beetle   centipede

cricket   mole cricket   butterfly   ant   bee   water strider

stick insect   water scorpion   firefly   cicada   tiger beetle

moth   horsefly   ant lion   water strider   giant water bug

fly   long-horned beetle   cockroach   scorpion   fly   scarab beetle   horsefly   jewel beetle

grasshopper   firefly   bee   water scorpion   ant   cicada

butterfly   ant lion   diving beetle   dragonfly   rhinoceros beetle   carabid beetle   katydid   locust

pill bug   drone beetle   mantis   ladybug

spider   stag beetle   carabid beetle   locust   jewel beetle   tiger beetle   millipede   cricket   scorpion   diving beetle   millipede   moth

50

Birds of a Feather
Stay Together (Matching 38)

Circle the matching birds.

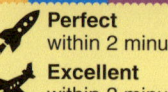 **Perfect** within 2 minutes	**Great** within 5 minutes	**Fair** within 10 minutes
Excellent within 3 minutes	**Very good** within 6 minutes	**Satisfactory** within 12 minutes
Super within 4 minutes	**Good** within 8 minutes	**Keep Trying** more than 12 minutes

DATE   NAME   TIME

eagle   turkey   macaw   hawk   woodpecker   owl   albatross   toucan   canary   penguin   condor

goose   wren   flamingo   skylark   quail   crow   chicken   mandarin duck   skylark   flamingo

Siberian blue robin   kingfisher   scops owl   pelican   magpie   cuckoo   hummingbird

condor   pigeon   swallow   peacock   swan   emu   duck   kingfisher   wild duck   sea gull   peacock

wild goose   penguin

albatross   toucan   crow   parrot   wild duck   sparrow   chicken   quail   pigeon   sparrow   parrot   swan

cuckoo   magpie   mandarin duck   duck   eagle   Siberian blue robin   wren   woodpecker   pelican   swallow   emu

canary

owl   hummingbird   ostrich   scops owl   sea gull   goose   macaw   hawk   ostrich   wild goose   turkey

51

Exploring the Zoo
(Matching 40)

	Perfect within 2 minutes		Great within 5 minutes		Fair within 10 minutes
	Excellent within 3 minutes		Very good within 6 minutes		Satisfactory within 12 minutes
	Super within 4 minutes		Good within 8 minutes		Keep Trying more than 12 minutes

■ Circle the matching animals.

DATE   NAME   TIME

giraffe

gorilla

rhinoceros

frog

elephant

tiger

crocodile

whale

wild boar

crocodile

squirrel

lion

bat

cheetah

sheep

wild boar

cow

sheep

pig

mouse

chimpanzee

bottlenose dolphin

tortoise

seal

frog

lion

cheetah

guinea pig

horse

mole

bear

gorilla

leopard

chameleon

fox

mouse

fox

tortoise

killer whale

panda

hippopotamus

seal

squirrel

pig

zebra

donkey

elephant

rabbit

zebra

deer

leopard

chameleon

guinea pig

hamster

killer whale

rabbit

polar bear

bear

koala

donkey

chimpanzee

hamster

cow

goat

kangaroo

polar bear

panda

kangaroo

whale

tiger

bottlenose dolphin

goat

giraffe

bat

mole

rhinoceros

horse

koala

deer

hippopotamus

Dive into the Water

(Matching 40)

■ Circle the matching fish.

	Perfect within 2 minutes		Great within 5 minutes		Fair within 10 minutes
	Excellent within 3 minutes		Very good within 6 minutes		Satisfactory within 12 minutes
	Super within 4 minutes		Good within 8 minutes		Keep Trying more than 12 minutes

DATE   NAME   TIME

yellow tail, humphead wrasse, blowfish, jack, hammerhead shark, sole, anglerfish, porcupine fish, bonito, scorpion fish, sea bream, manta ray, arowana, shark, coelacanth, cod fish, sunfish, piranha, loach, porcupine fish, flatfish, parrot fish, shark, salmon, ray, angelfish, anchovy, flying fish, goldfish, ray, cutlassfish, black bass, angelfish, scorpion fish, herring, flying fish, sunfish, sole, carp, electric eel, tuna, anglerfish, loach, king salmon, moray, coelacanth, sea horse, arowana, eel, humphead wrasse, cod fish, jack, sea bream, cutlassfish, black bass, parrot fish, anchovy, flatfish, salmon, goldfish, tuna, piranha, catfish, moray, king salmon, carp, flatfish, swordfish, sea horse, rainbow trout, manta ray, hammerhead shark, swordfish, rainbow trout, yellow tail, bonito, eel, sea horse, electric eel, herring, blowfish, catfish

53 At the Farmer's Market (Matching 40)

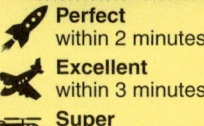

Perfect within 2 minutes	**Great** within 5 minutes	**Fair** within 10 minutes
Excellent within 3 minutes	**Very good** within 6 minutes	**Satisfactory** within 12 minutes
Super within 4 minutes	**Good** within 8 minutes	**Keep Trying** more than 12 minutes

Circle the matching produce.

DATE NAME TIME

red pepper
grape
peach
pea
cucumber
raspberry
broccoli
apple
jalapeno pepper
asparagus
cabbage
banana
melon
potato
grapefruit
zucchini
fig
tomato
cauliflower
dragon fruit
orange
kiwifruit
cherry
eggplant
strawberry
corn
durian
walnut
cucumber
pear
blueberry
celery
tomato
dragon fruit
cauliflower
cherry
blueberry
lemon
green pepper
asparagus
corn
walnut
prune
lemon
strawberry
grape
potato
turnip
onion
orange
banana
zucchini
turnip
onion
durian
green pepper
melon
fig
kiwifruit
carrot
pea
apricot
eggplant
jalapeno pepper
peach
apricot
cabbage
lettuce
broccoli
pineapple
carrot
raspberry
lettuce
celery
apple
red pepper
pineapple
grapefruit
prune
pear

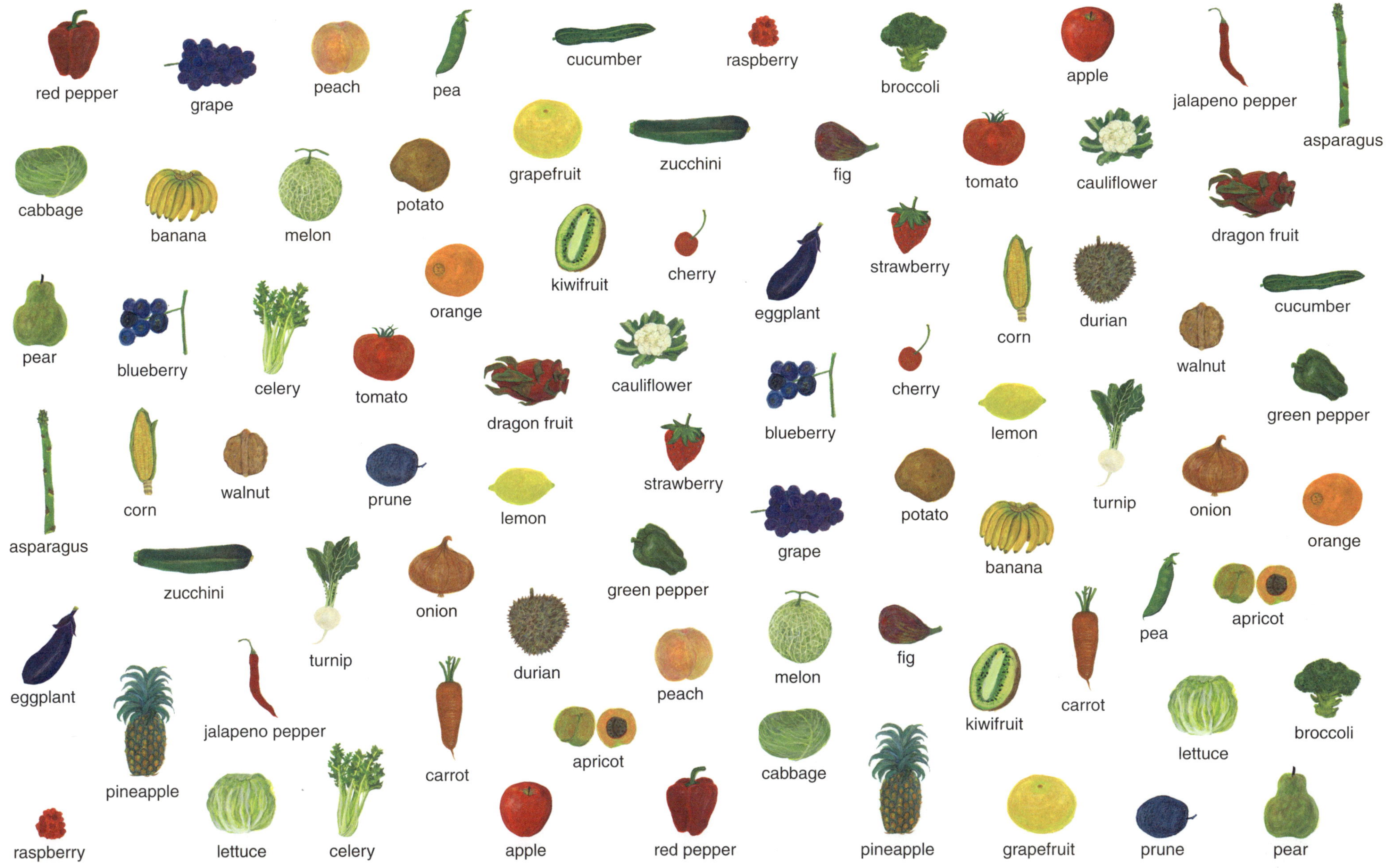

■ Circle the matching flowers.

Perfect within 2 minutes	**Great** within 5 minutes	**Fair** within 10 minutes
Excellent within 3 minutes	**Very good** within 6 minutes	**Satisfactory** within 12 minutes
Super within 4 minutes	**Good** within 8 minutes	**Keep Trying** more than 12 minutes

DATE   NAME   TIME

Catch the Bug

(Matching 40)

Circle the matching insects.

DATE · NAME · TIME

spider · tiger beetle · carabid beetle · rhinoceros beetle · katydid · stag beetle · wasp · stick insect · cricket · long-horned beetle

giant water bug · centipede · cockroach · dragonfly · mantis · millipede

water scorpion · butterfly · dragonfly · drone beetle · diving beetle

ladybug · stick insect · diving beetle · pill bug · scorpion · cricket · jewel beetle · ant lion · bee · cricket · scorpion

scarab beetle · cicada · mantis · ant · fly · horsefly · firefly · locust · jewel beetle · earwig · grasshopper · mole cricket

stag beetle · moth · wasp · drone beetle · jewel beetle · bee · rhinoceros beetle · water strider · butterfly · scarab beetle

grasshopper · pill bug · ant · cicada · fly · ladybug

horsefly · cricket · ant lion · locust · mole cricket · tiger beetle · giant water bug · katydid · moth

long-horned beetle · earwig · firefly · butterfly · water strider · millipede · spider · cockroach · centipede · butterfly · water scorpion · carabid beetle

Birds of a Feather Stay Together (Matching 40)

■ Circle the matching birds.

	Perfect within 2 minutes		Great within 5 minutes		Fair within 10 minutes
	Excellent within 3 minutes		Very good within 6 minutes		Satisfactory within 12 minutes
	Super within 4 minutes		Good within 8 minutes		Keep Trying more than 12 minutes

DATE   NAME   TIME

penguin

ptarmigan

skylark

magpie

duck

flamingo

mandarin duck

owl

peacock

canary

parrot

ostrich

sparrow

chicken

quail

woodpecker

toucan

goose

wren

cuckoo

scops owl

condor

eagle

scops owl

sea gull

swallow

macaw

swan

hawk

emu

Siberian blue robin

sea gull

turkey

parrot

wild goose

condor

goose

albatross

cuckoo

sparrow

swallow

crow

skylark

pelican

wild duck

owl

emu

peacock

wild duck

crow

quail

albatross

guinea fowl

pigeon

wild goose

chicken

Siberian blue robin

pigeon

turkey

pelican

hummingbird

magpie

kingfisher

wren

swan

eagle

woodpecker

duck

ostrich

kingfisher

guinea fowl

macaw

hawk

penguin

ptarmigan

canary

flamingo

toucan

mandarin duck

hummingbird

All Objects (Matching 40)

■ Circle the matching objects.

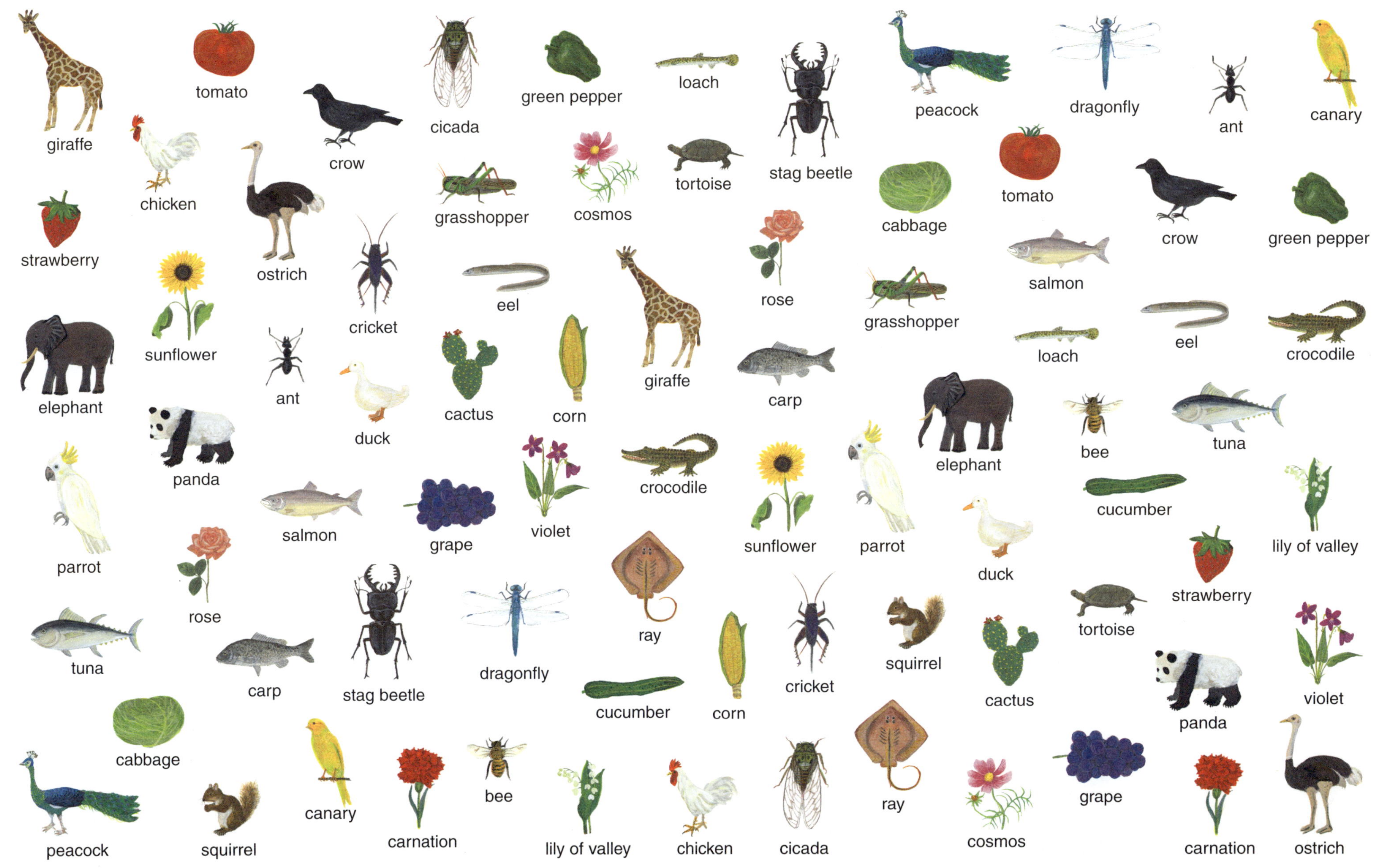

DATE	NAME	TIME

giraffe

tomato

crow

cicada

green pepper

loach

stag beetle

peacock

dragonfly

ant

canary

chicken

grasshopper

cosmos

tortoise

cabbage

tomato

crow

green pepper

strawberry

ostrich

cricket

eel

rose

salmon

grasshopper

salmon

loach

eel

crocodile

sunflower

ant

giraffe

carp

loach

elephant

duck

cactus

corn

crocodile

sunflower

parrot

elephant

bee

tuna

panda

salmon

grape

violet

crocodile

sunflower

parrot

duck

cucumber

lily of valley

parrot

rose

ray

strawberry

tuna

carp

stag beetle

dragonfly

cucumber

corn

cricket

squirrel

tortoise

panda

violet

cabbage

canary

bee

lily of valley

chicken

cicada

ray

cosmos

grape

carnation

ostrich

peacock

squirrel

carnation

58 All Objects (Matching 40)

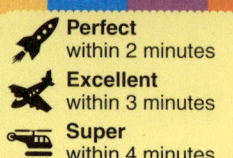

Perfect within 2 minutes
Excellent within 3 minutes
Super within 4 minutes
Great within 5 minutes
Very good within 6 minutes
Good within 8 minutes
Fair within 10 minutes
Satisfactory within 12 minutes
Keep Trying more than 12 minutes

Circle the matching objects.

DATE NAME TIME

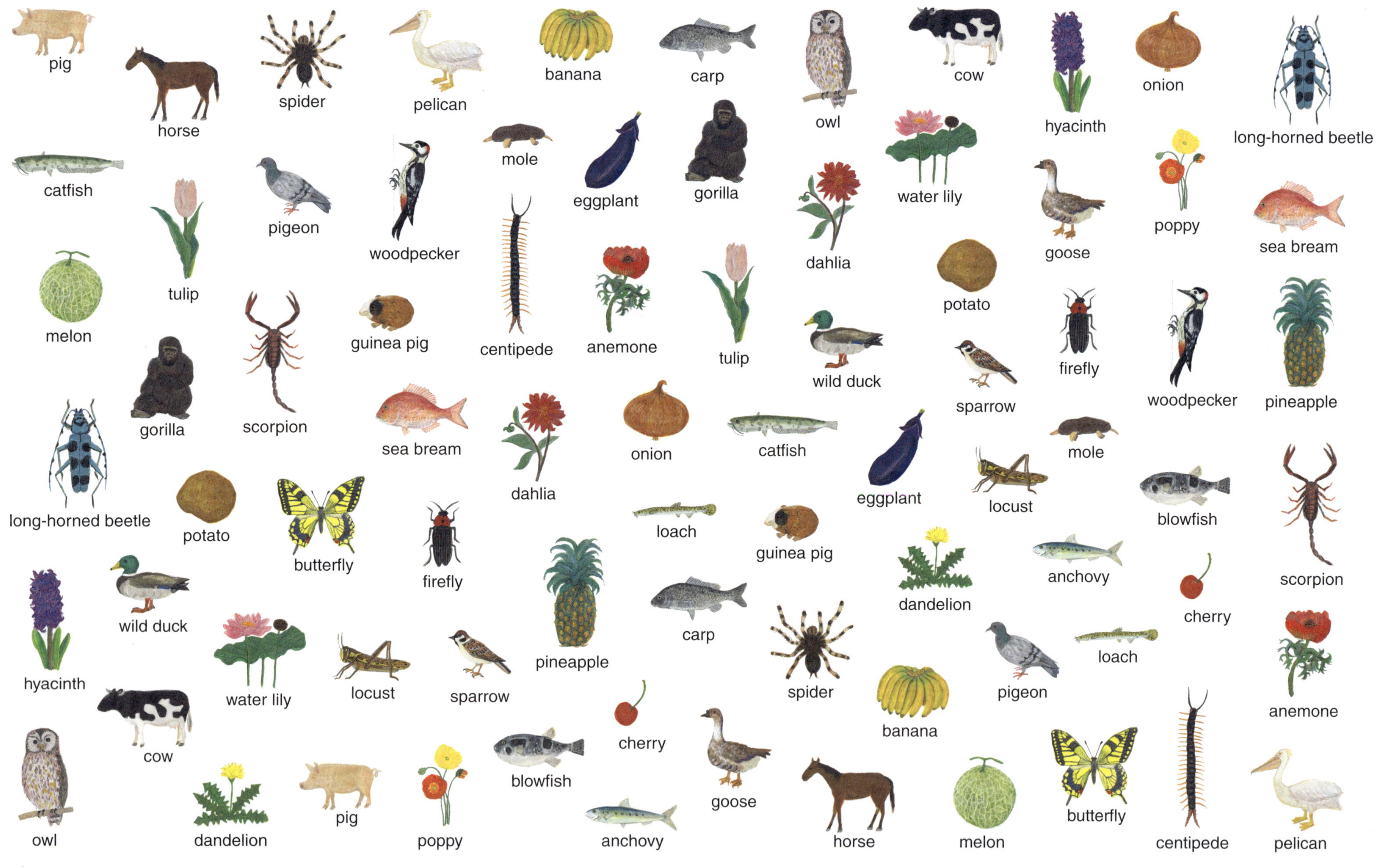
pig
horse
spider
pelican
banana
carp
owl
cow
hyacinth
onion
long-horned beetle
catfish
pigeon
woodpecker
mole
eggplant
gorilla
water lily
dahlia
goose
poppy
sea bream
melon
tulip
guinea pig
centipede
anemone
tulip
wild duck
potato
firefly
sparrow
woodpecker
pineapple
long-horned beetle
gorilla
scorpion
sea bream
dahlia
onion
catfish
eggplant
locust
mole
blowfish
scorpion
potato
butterfly
firefly
loach
guinea pig
dandelion
anchovy
cherry
pineapple
hyacinth
wild duck
water lily
locust
sparrow
carp
spider
loach
pigeon
anemone
banana
owl
cow
dandelion
pig
poppy
blowfish
cherry
anchovy
goose
horse
melon
butterfly
centipede
pelican

All Objects (Matching 40)

	Perfect within 2 minutes		Great within 5 minutes		Fair within 10 minutes
	Excellent within 3 minutes		Very good within 6 minutes		Satisfactory within 12 minutes
	Super within 4 minutes		Good within 8 minutes		Keep Trying more than 12 minutes

■ Circle the matching objects.

DATE   NAME   TIME

eagle

pear

magpie

rabbit

angelfish

turkey

asparagus

salvia

anglerfish

chrysanthemum

peach

penguin

cherry blossoms

lemon

rhinoceros

zebra

eagle

wild boar

apricot

clover

mole cricket

bonito

rabbit

lettuce

katydid

rhinoceros

flying fish

cockroach

fox

gerbera

marguerite

chrysanthemum

rhinoceros beetle

sea horse

cockroach

jewel beetle

magpie

cricket

kiwifruit

water strider

mouse

sea gull

mouse

turkey

lettuce

kingfisher

penguin

salvia

cricket

anglerfish

pear

peach

angelfish

katydid

goldfish

lily

hawk

water strider

fox

gerbera

marguerite

lemon

hawk

flying fish

kingfisher

sea horse

jewel beetle

goldfish

apricot

kiwifruit

lily

bonito

rhinoceros beetle

cherry blossoms

mole cricket

asparagus

clover

wild boar

sea gull

zebra

Circle the matching objects.

 Perfect within 2 minutes	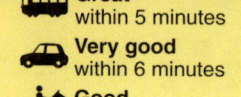 Great within 5 minutes	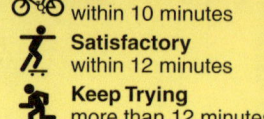 Fair within 10 minutes
Excellent within 3 minutes	Very good within 6 minutes	Satisfactory within 12 minutes
Super within 4 minutes	Good within 8 minutes	Keep Trying more than 12 minutes

DATE   NAME   TIME

hippopotamus
flamingo
sunfish
forget-me-not
carabid beetle
arowana
grapefruit
leopard
bear
amaryllis

celery
flamingo
ladybug
tiger
gladiolus
stock
walnut
fly
carrot
scorpion fish

scops owl
ant lion
lion
apple
scops owl
wild goose
diving beetle
clematis
broccoli
swordfish

black bass
amaryllis
moth
frog
fly
black bass
mandarin duck
carabid beetle
shark
anthurium

anthurium
carrot
scorpion fish
swan
walnut
fig
forget-me-not
toucan
swan
hippopotamus
lion

toucan
wild goose
mandarin duck
arowana
ant lion
toucan
pansy
pill bug

pansy
grapefruit
pill bug
clematis
broccoli
swallow
moth
ladybug
stock
fig

leopard
swordfish
bear
diving beetle
shark
sunfish
celery
gladiolus
flamingo
frog
apple

swallow
tiger

All Objects (Matching 40)

■ Circle the matching objects.

Perfect within 2 minutes	**Great** within 5 minutes	**Fair** within 10 minutes
Excellent within 3 minutes	**Very good** within 6 minutes	**Satisfactory** within 12 minutes
Super within 4 minutes	**Good** within 8 minutes	**Keep Trying** more than 12 minutes

DATE   NAME   TIME

coelacanth

cheetah

sweet pea

kangaroo

magnolia

blueberry

sole

persian buttercup

iris

durian

poinsettia

quail

cuckoo

deer

orange

drone beetle

cauliflower

Siberian blue robin

turnip

peach

emu

skylark

hammerhead shark

cauliflower

koala

horsefly

skylark

cornflower

mantis

condor

stick insect

water scorpion

orange

goat

horsefly

pea

scarab beetle

giant water bug

water scorpion

pea

scarab beetle

cornflower

cutlassfish

poinsettia

porcupine fish

cod fish

chimpanzee

persian buttercup

condor

cod fish

cuckoo

stick insect

albatross

sweet pea

deer

hammerhead shark

dragon fruit

sole

durian

porcupine fish

cutlassfish

drone beetle

mantis

dragon fruit

kangaroo

emu

quail

goat

giant water bug

iris

turnip

koala

blueberry

peach

coelacanth

chimpanzee

magnolia

cheetah

albatross

Siberian blue robin

All Objects (Matching 40)

Circle the matching objects.

DATE   NAME   TIME

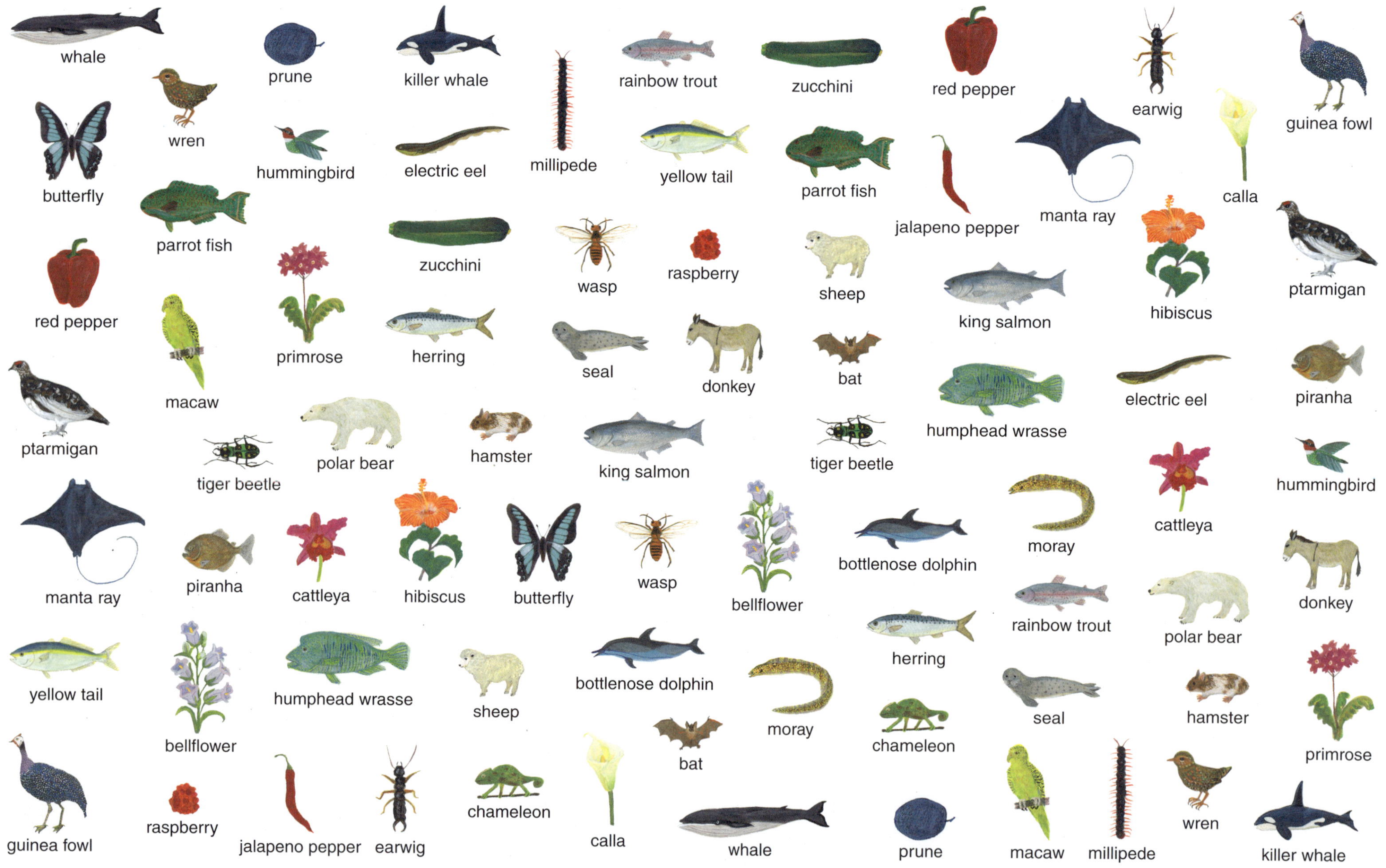

whale

prune

killer whale

rainbow trout

zucchini

red pepper

earwig

guinea fowl

butterfly

wren

hummingbird

electric eel

millipede

yellow tail

parrot fish

manta ray

calla

parrot fish

zucchini

wasp

raspberry

sheep

jalapeno pepper

hibiscus

ptarmigan

red pepper

macaw

primrose

herring

seal

donkey

bat

king salmon

electric eel

piranha

ptarmigan

tiger beetle

polar bear

hamster

king salmon

tiger beetle

humphead wrasse

hummingbird

manta ray

piranha

cattleya

hibiscus

butterfly

wasp

bellflower

bottlenose dolphin

moray

cattleya

donkey

yellow tail

humphead wrasse

sheep

bottlenose dolphin

herring

rainbow trout

polar bear

bellflower

chameleon

seal

hamster

guinea fowl

raspberry

jalapeno pepper

earwig

chameleon

calla

bat

moray

whale

prune

macaw

millipede

wren

primrose

killer whale